A Year in E

By

Simon de Wulf

Simondewulf.com

Copyright © 2022 Simon de Wulf

All rights reserved.

Preface

This is a tale of our stay in Barbados to escape the UK's lockdown in 2021. It's based on a blog I published throughout the year and charts our adventures and experiences of island life in the Caribbean.

Our story transcends a little more than a year but 'A year and a half in Barbados' doesn't quite have the same ring to it as the current title!

1

Prologue

The UK Government announced its first nationwide Coronavirus lockdown on 23 March 2020 fearing the widespread effects of the disease. This was a serious blow for many particularly those who were retired like myself and used to travelling freely.

Restrictions eased towards the end of June and in July, I invited my girlfriend, Antonina, a Ukrainian, to join me in England. We managed to get and about, see some sights and utilised the 'Eat Out to Help Out' scheme, which offered a 50% discount on meals up to £10 per person.

With more restrictions looming - a 'rule of six' for indoor and outdoor gatherings, a return to working from home and a 10pm curfew for the hospitality sector – and thinking the continent might be freer we decided to embark on a road trip to Europe. This would avoid negotiating the difficulties associated with flying and would give us greater flexibility in how and where we travelled.

At the beginning of September, we left the UK to drive down to Portugal. We took Le Shuttle, one of only a handful of vehicles on board, and despite essentially ignoring Foreign Office travel advice had no problems leaving the UK with the French not seemingly interested in our arrival on their soil either. The roads were empty and there were no

Brits that we could see at a time of year when France would be full of them.

We drove down through France and for our first night stayed with friends who owned a chateau near Saumur. En route, we stopped off in Giverny to visit Monet's house and gardens which were beautiful.

We then headed for Angouleme, an ancient fortified town, spending the night there before heading for Biarritz and St Jean de Luz on the southwest coast. The French were out in force and there was no social distancing on Biarritz beach where they were packed in like sardines, soaking up the rays.

We explored the old town, had a meal in a Basque restaurant and stayed the night in a very modern boutique hotel.

We then entered Spain and drove down through the Basque Country skirting Bilbao and striking diagonally across Spain towards Portugal which we entered close to Badajoz, scene of a historic siege and bloody victory for Wellington's army in the Peninsular War in 1812. The British lost a third of their forces in the assault, some 5,000 British soldiers out of 15,000. Afterwards Wellington wrote to Lord Liverpool, the British prime minister, "The capture of Badajoz affords as strong an instance of the gallantry of our troops as has ever been displayed, but I anxiously hope that I shall never again

be the instrument of putting them to such a test as that to which they were put last night."

We then drove through the ancient town of Evora before arriving in Monchique on the evening of 5 September.

We had temperatures of between 28 and 34 degrees C all the way though the car temperature gauge touched 40 in the middle of Spain. I was worried that my twenty-year-old Rover 75 would overheat but it performed faultlessly. It is a great car to cruise continental motorways in. I did have it thoroughly checked over before we set off and some tints applied to the rear windows of the car to minimise sun infiltration.

Once in Monchique we had a month of blisteringly hot weather, unusual for the mountain region there, and enjoyed the villa's pool and exploring the local neighbourhood. We also discovered a beautiful golf course nearby called Espiche and played there three times.

Antonina had never been to Portugal so she found it interesting. We also looked at properties as I have always had a yen to live there but prices had risen as locals and foreigners were looking to escape to more rural locations to get away from Covid.

After four weeks there we decided to prolong our stay and decamped to a villa outside Sao Bras de Alportel for a further two weeks to explore the Eastern side of the Algarve which is an area I did not know well.

We headed up the river along the Spanish border to Alcoutim before heading west inland through the mountains and some pretty rural out of the way places. We played golf at Monte Rei, Portugal's number one golf course, and one of the best in Europe. The concierge service was fantastic and the course equally good.

The additional two weeks went quickly and then it was time to leave. We decided to head back up the East coast of Spain and through Eastern France; a longer way back but we wanted to enjoy the warm weather for as long as possible.

Our first night was supposed to be in a small hotel in Playas de Vera, a seaside town on the south east coast of Spain. We fronted up at the hotel to find it in darkness. It was closed. So much for booking.com. There seemed to be little else that was open so we headed for Vera, a larger settlement on a hill top nearby. It was 9pm and we were starving and needed to eat. If needs must we would sleep in the car.

We found a café that was open and the proprietor said he could rustle up an omelette as the kitchen was closed.

As we discussed our plight a short, handsome, though tough looking man off to our right spoke to us.

'I couldn't help but overhear your conversation, are you stuck for somewhere to stay?'

This was delivered in a cockney accent. The man was a Londoner.

'Yes,' we replied.

'My name is Jack and I live locally. I have a spare room. You can stay with me.'

We chatted some more and accepted his invitation. Although in his early fifties he appeared retired but there was something unnerving about him which was amplified when we set foot in his house to see photographs of boxers adorning the walls, a picture of a group of hard looking men gathered around a bar and two bull mastiffs which jumped up at us on entry.

Jack had been an amateur boxer and made enough money in London to retire to Spain. He had gangster written all over him, though I am not really qualified to judge.

He showed us the house including a den which contained a large punch bag suspended from the ceiling. He went into a crouch and gave it several vicious punches before relaxing and asking us if we needed a drink before retiring. We declined and headed for bed. Neither of us slept well as the dogs prowled the corridor outside our room. We determined to leave early, leaving him a thank you note.

We arose at 5.30, dressed quietly and slipped down to the kitchen and the back door. The dogs were mercifully asleep.

As we tiptoed into the kitchen, we were greeted with a hearty welcome.

'Good morning. Up early?'

I recovered my poise and stammered that we had a long way to go and needed to be on way.

'Nonsense,' Jack replied. 'You will need tea and a good breakfast. I'll have some eggs on in a jiffy with some bacon and beans.'

Both of us were unnerved but I managed to insist that we had to be going, thanking him profusely for his hospitality and for taking us in. Maybe he was lonely and needed some company but we were glad to be out of there and heading north.

Our second night saw us stopping off in a seaside town called Sitges near Barcelona. I had never heard of it but it was a beautiful place, very similar to Nice but much smaller. Our hotel room overlooked the beach and we decided to stay for three days particularly as there was an old established golf course nearby.

I also enjoyed taking in the Spanish ladies on the beach from our hotel window. The French ladies seemed to have abandoned going topless but not the Spanish women and one particularly stately beauty sat naked on a nearby outcrop of rock most days.

But all good things come to an end and it was then off northwards through Barcelona to Andorra, a strange little country run jointly by Spain and France which appeared to be a duty-free zone high up in the mountains; incredible Pyrenees Mountain scenery but we didn't like the main town.

We then descended into France which was a little hairy here and there and my brakes smelled of burnt fibre when we arrived on the plain. The descent was not helped by counting at least six cars that had come to grief on the twisty road, never mind the wrecked automobiles we couldn't see in the steep ravines!

We stayed in Carcassonne that night, an attractive medieval town now a UNESCO World Heritage site. It was then on to Lyon.

I said to Antonina 'find us a town on the map that is smallish and off the beaten track for the night,' trying to avoid the major towns and cities and Covid.'

'Beane' she said, '21,000 people and in the middle of nowhere.'

'Great,' I thought until we entered the outer precincts and counted at least five well-known hotel brands.

In the quaint cobbled centre, we pulled over and had a coffee and within ten minutes three Maseratis and two Ferraris had driven by.

'Where are we I thought?' I looked it up on Google to discover we were in the 'capital' and heart of the Burgundy winemaking area. Beane was a fashionable destination and very much an 'it' place to be; never mind the wine.

Of course, this meant Beane was expensive and we did well to find a garret of a gite above a wine bar on the edge of town for the night.

It was then off north and we ended up in Montreuil, another pretty medieval fortified town close to Calais and Le Touquet which had a well-known golf course. I needed one more game under my belt before crossing the Channel and two weeks quarantine. We stayed two nights there and then crossed to England. No problems or questioning on re-entry either.

We then went into self-isolation for two weeks and just as I was looking forward to getting back on the golf course the rain came down for ten straight days.

We had thought of setting off on another road trip to Turkey and spending Christmas there but some of the countries we would have to pass through appeared to be implementing quarantine for travellers and with a worsening global Covid situation decided to stay put.

Boris Johnson, the UK's prime minister, then announced a second lockdown on 31 October which ended on 2 December. But during December there were rumours that we would enter a third lockdown in early January, so golf would be off the agenda for the foreseeable future and we would be marooned indoors during the dark months of January, February and probably March.

Being an adventurer, I made the decision we should decamp to the Caribbean, Barbados, for twelve months to avoid the lockdown and the British winter.

The primary income earner for Barbados is tourism and that tanked once Covid arrived so some bright spark, later I was given to understand it might have been the prime minister, Mia Mottley, came up with the idea of the Barbados Welcome Stamp, essentially a 12-month visa designed to attract those who are retired or can work remotely. I jumped at it, applied, got accepted and we booked our flights.

We arrived at Terminal 2 Heathrow at 8.25am on the 2nd

of January to board our flight. However, even though we allowed more than two hours it was all bit of a rush with the added Covid validation procedures and we just made the flight. The plane was a Dreamliner and very smooth and comfortable. We were in economy but there were plenty of empty seats so could stretch out. There were lots of native Bajans on board either returning home or going on holiday and their discipline in terms of mask wearing was not the best. Still, we took comfort from the fact everyone on board had been Covid tested prior to embarkation until I remembered reading in the media about some oik from Birmingham who was selling fake PCR certificates on the web and making a small fortune!

We touched down in Barbados an hour early at 2.30pm local time. The warmth hit us as we left the aircraft and the humid air smelt different to that of the Far East. But it was good to be in sunshine and heat. While the flight was painless, we had to jump through several hoops exiting the airport; mainly Covid related.

We took a Covid approved taxi and arrived for a week's quarantine in a government approved hotel apartment at the cheaper end of the spectrum but it was functional and clean. We then relaxed on the hotel balcony watching the sun set with a beer in hand and wearing only shorts and a polo shirt in my case. This was better than the cool grey of England.

The name of the local beer is Banks, very drinkable and I wondered if it was any relation to the Banks' bitter, I used to drink at university in Birmingham!

We could see the sea off to our left and it was 26 degrees with a cooling breeze. We couldn't quite believe we were in Barbados and both decided we could get used to this.

4 January 2021

We have been in Barbados for two days and had our second Covid test this morning which was a chaotic affair.

We were taken by taxi to a local testing clinic and queued outside for an hour and went where we were told. But there was no pathway control as the exit was the same as the entrance and they muddled up our names but it all got straightened out in the end. We should get our results within 72 hours.

We are confined to our room at Carib Blue Apartments. But everyone is helpful and we rely on Christine, who runs the attached restaurant, to bring us breakfasts and supplies.

When she pulls up in the car park outside, we shout down a 'good morning' and place our orders. Fortunately, we brought some frozen packed meals with us plus other food essentials and can rustle up a meal in the apartment's kitchenette.

There is a curfew in place from 9.00pm to 5.00am, to stop late night beach gatherings, parties and the like, but people are free to move around otherwise. Some bars and restaurants are closed but I guessed that was more to do with the lack of tourists. The sea looks very inviting from where we sit on our balcony; all shades of aquamarine blue and we are

looking forward to having a dip.

Meanwhile, one of us, at least, carries out her daily exercise regimen on the balcony.

A car is one thing we are going to have to acquire and, as a car nut interested in older cars, I got very excited when a white thirty-year old E32, a seven series BMW, appeared in the hotel car park below!

7 January 2021

We were released from quarantine this afternoon after our second Covid tests proved negative and promptly left the hotel and went for a walk to explore the environs around Dover Beach, our current location.

The sea, almost a peacock blue, looked straight out of a holiday brochure and beach side restaurants looked inviting. Needless to say, after a lengthy walk, we fell into one such beachside bar and had a couple of margaritas and something to eat overlooking a white sandy beach, turquoise sea, palms swaying in the breeze and watching the sun set into the sea. And with happy hour we were feeling very chilled on such a balmy evening!

Apart from mask wearing, distancing etc, life appears normal with places open apart from some which serve the tourist trade and have shut for economic reasons. Having said that there seem to be both Brits and Americans here on holiday though a handful by comparison to normal times.

Covid cases are few, though rising, and the authorities seem to have a good grip on the situation.

8 January 2021

Today we check out of Carib Blue Apartments and move to an AirBnb apartment in Kendal, St John, a different, more remote and inland locale in the east of country. First, we needed to hire a car.

The hotel arranged for us to be taken to a local concern where I met Umer, a Guajarati, who hailed from Gloucester in the UK originally. Being retired and now an impecunious writer, we needed something cheap and cheerful and an elderly blue Suzuki Swift with 227,000 kilometres on the clock fitted the bill.

It amused me to see a sticker on the rear windscreen

denoting it had initially been supplied by Colin Appleyard Cars of Keighley in West Yorkshire!

Barbados being originally a British colony they drive on the left so at least that would be familiar though I wondered why the car sported a Kilometre per hour speed dial.

I was also fast coming to the realisation that as an island everything must be either flown or shipped in, an expensive proposition, so they re-use and make everything last as long as possible with cars no exception. At the budget end many of the cars are old and a jigsaw of metal panels held together with welds, screws and plastic cable ties but, they survive and handle the roads - a testament to the original manufacturers almost singularly Japanese.

So, with our luggage on board, we set off for Kendal in the rural parish of St John towards the east, Atlantic side of the island using a traditional map. The countryside was green and full of sugar cane fields. The scenery was a pleasant contrast to the more urban coast though not as idyllic as the blue Caribbean Sea framed by swaying palms and white beaches.

Though it was early days, what also struck us was the unfinished and relatively dilapidated state of many of the timber and breeze block properties we passed decorated in several cases by rusting heaps of aged cars. But they love their use of colour! Many buildings were a mixture of bright greens, reds, blues and yellows!

We stopped for lunch at a local, rural, restaurant where they served an excellent barbequed marlin with salad and fries. The roads in the hinterland are a lot worse than those in the more densely populated coastal areas but the car took them in its stride.

We eventually arrived at our apartment in Kendal and settled in. After the hotel the apartment was spacious and looked out over green countryside. This would do us until we found longer term rental accommodation.

However, one of the first things we noticed out here was the number of mosquitoes so after being bitten a few times a plug-in mosquito fumigator and a couple of coils were the first things entered on a shopping list.

We finally retired for the night and fell asleep listening to a new noise, not cicadas but the singing of tiny whistling frogs – the sound of the night in Barbados.

9 January 2021

We woke up early and as a golfer, who had been deprived of golf for some weeks, it was time to explore one of the local courses. The nearest is Barbados Golf Club, a Ron Kirby designed course in the south of the island. We arrived early, signed in and had a beer while waiting for our early afternoon tee time. We took a golf cart as the course was unfamiliar to us. The fairways appeared in good condition and the greens were slick; a little too quick for me as this stage. I played the front nine well but things slipped after that but it was great to be out playing golf!

With the sun descending the final holes and mature trees and green fairways were bathed in a warm light and a par three over some water looked like a signature hole.

Afterwards we headed off for a Mexican dinner at a venue we had spotted the previous day by the beach.

After dinner, and several Margaritas, the road home was somewhat exciting! Google Maps took us through the middle of a sugar cane plantation. With cane leaves brushing the car on both sides, sizeable rocks jutting out of the track and deep puddles of rain water I wondered where we would end up. However, the Suzuki Swift took it in its stride and, luckily, we eventually emerged onto a tarmac road. I laughed afterwards though at the time it was a little tense!

19 January 2021

It's been twelve days since we were released from quarantine and we have been pretty active in terms of leisure activities and looking for a longer-term rental property to stay in.

We have swum in the sea off Dover Beach, had lunch at Mullins above a lovely beach on the West coast and visited two other beaches. Very little beats lying back on a lounger just feet from the sea, watching the sun set with a beer in hand on a balmy evening.

Coming from Eastbourne in East Sussex, England, I was amused to see that the beach area we tend to frequent has surrounding areas called Worthing, Brighton, Hastings and Marine Gardens with a stretch of coast named Beachy Head.

We have also played golf at two courses in the southern part of the island. I am dying to try the Old Nine and the Country Club courses at Sandy Lane and the Royal Westmoreland. But securing a longer-term rental property is the priority at the moment. The agents we have met have been active and helpful and we have identified three we like. But, as always, each comes with a compromise.

We visited a local supermarket at Six Roads for the first time and I was surprised and delighted to see some familiar Tesco own label products and Heinz baked beans! The one local variety we tried was odd to say the least. There is no doubt prices are at between one and half to three times what we would pay back home in the UK. So, we will need to exercise some discipline when we do our food shop.

We visited the Sheraton Mall to source a local SIM card and a few other things and while impressed with the Covid precautions – temperature taken on entry and insistence on using hand sanitiser – we found having to take hand sanitiser on entry to every store a little hard wearing on the hands.

Despite buying fumigators and coils we continue to be bitten by small mosquitoes which are hard to see and hear unlike the UK variety or those I have encountered in the Far East. Its Dengue season so we need to be careful and we are more worried about contracting this than Covid. The symptoms, apparently, are the same!

The climate continues to be very pleasant with a constant breeze from the easterly trade winds keeping us cool.

21 January 2021

Where to stay in Barbados?

We are getting to know the southern half of the island pretty well and have narrowed down our long-term property search to three properties. One is on the West coast close to Fitts beach. It's a town house in a pleasant gated complex only minutes from the sea and a local supermarket. The complex is full of gracious old trees and vibrant shrubbery and comes with a pool.

The second is within the Rockley Golf club complex and originally designed for visitors on vacation. The terrace on the ground floor overlooks the eighteenth green and is surrounded by mature trees. It's a very pleasant place to sit and the complex also has a pool.

The third is a detached house some way inland in a quiet neighbourhood. The house is very spacious and has a magnificent verandah with views of the sea and open country behind. We liked it and will attempt to secure this property.

In between our property searches we have managed to have lunch at a beautiful boutique hotel overlooking Miami Beach and at an Italian restaurant only feet from the sea at Fitts beach. The food at the former was excellent. The food at the latter awful but more than made up for by its wonderful location.

We decided to play a round of golf at Rockley Golf Club which turned into a lot of monkey business.

Just as I was about to tee off on the 5th a group of monkeys jumped down from the tree overhead. Maybe they were interested in my banana shaped drive! I could see one eyeing up my Titleist Pro V1 golf ball. Don't even think about it mate, I thought. A Topflight ball fine but not a Pro V1. After some chattering, they loped off.

We finished the day by having a swim in the sea and sipping Margaritas on Dover Beach watching the sun set. This place is magical but then I guess so are all the islands in the Caribbean.

As we do every evening when we have been out, we head

home to our apartment in Kendal, St John, to be welcomed by the dog, chickens and goats. Not ours I hasten to add but property of the owner of the house.

We are getting used to life in the countryside here.

25 January 2021

Life is a beach

We decided to explore the Atlantic coast side of the island and on separate days discovered two wonderful beaches called Bottom Bay and Peat Bay.

The access to Bottom Bay beach wasn't immediately obvious but we found the steps down almost hidden by undergrowth and descended through a tunnel of foliage to emerge onto a white sandy beach with a deep cave hewn out of the coral off to the right.

I didn't know this but the island was formed less than one million years ago with the collision of the Atlantic crustal and Caribbean tectonic plates, along with a volcanic eruption. Coral then formed, accumulating to approximately 300 feet. It is geologically unique with the underlying 'rock' structure being coral. For palaeontologists interested in fossils it's heaven as one can pick up shells deep inland and clearly see fossil remains of all kinds embedded in the coral.

Unlike the placid Caribbean Sea of the west coast, the sea on the Atlantic side is constantly moving with sizeable waves and having decided to take the plunge I was struck by how fierce the undertow was and how powerful the waves were.

'I'm getting too old for this kind of swimming,' I thought to myself and think I will keep my bathing confined to the west coast!

But the sea was a beautiful colour, the sand white and with the easterly trade winds coming in off the sea we passed a pleasurable afternoon swimming and relaxing under the shade of the palm trees.

Peat Bay was even harder to find and necessitated negotiating an uneven grassy track till one came to a clear area directly above the beach on the cliff top, but the little Suzuki Swift handled it well. This place was as stunning as Bottom Bay, smaller, more desolate and there was no-one there; maybe because it was a weekday but I imagine the locals visit it at weekends. We descended several metres down narrow steps cut out of the coral cliff.

I imagined Robinson Crusoe discovered this kind of beach on his island which he named 'The Island of Despair'. Nothing to despair about here as civilisation is not far away!

We looked in awe at the beautiful blue waves rolling in up the empty white beach and smelt the sea on the breeze.

However, swimming was not possible as the underlying sand was dotted with ridges of coral. But it was a great place to relax and get into the water up to one's thighs.

Following this we enjoyed a late lunch at a pleasant restaurant called Cutters near Crane beach. We sat outside in the shade of a Magnolia Grandiflora tree sipping Rum punches and eating flying fish and chicken roti.

28 January 2021

A healthier climate

We decided to visit the historic centre of Bridgetown, the capital of Barbados, including George Washington House.

George Washington only ever left the American mainland once and that was for a trip to Barbados in 1751. Why you may ask? His elder half-brother Lawrence was suffering from tuberculosis and he was advised to spend the winter in the tropics to help his condition so George accompanied him. He was accommodated in a handsome early 18th century house belonging to a Captain Croftan, that had commanding views of Carlyle Bay and the Caribbean Sea. He was nineteen at the time and the trip left an indelible imprint on him in more ways than one.

I have only been here for four weeks but I have noticed a positive change in my health. My, admittedly limited, arthritis has improved, my joints move more freely, my rhinitis has diminished and my hair, nails and skin look a lot better. England is a wonderful country but the short, grey, cold and damp winter days have always affected me physically as well as mentally. So, I feel our decision to decamp here in January has definitely been vindicated from a health perspective not to mention escaping lockdown and the privations that brings.

As for George, his exposure to the British military organisation in Barbados, colonial officials, judges, merchants and planters and the fact that he was well received and entertained had a deep impact on, and shaped, his future aspirations. After returning to Virginia, unlike most of his colonial militia contemporaries, he sought a commission in the regular British army and that was the beginning of his revolutionary career.

However, despite enjoying the climate in Barbados, ironically, he also contracted small pox, then rampant in the world at the time and one of the most dreaded viral diseases of the 18th century. He made a full recovery and the antibodies he acquired gave him immunity when the disease frequently ravaged his army during the future revolutionary war.

So, no excuses for me not to capitalise on the wonderful climate, lose some weight and get fit through regular swimming, golf and general exercise. I can't lay the blame on the cold, wet weather for keeping me inside and not getting on with it!

George Washington House was closed due to Covid but it is pleasantly situated. The area is now a UNESCO World heritage site and includes the former Military prison which is now the Barbados historical museum. The cell block is still intact and one can imagine the 18th century British squaddie cooped up, two to a cell, sowing canvas while they awaited the outcome of sentencing for their misdemeanours.

29 January 2021

A beach life

I spoke too soon about escaping the UK lockdown and enjoying the freedom of movement in Barbados.

The Prime Minister of Barbados, the Honourable Mia Mottley, QC, MP, has addressed the island nation on TV and social media. With a total of 1,400 cases, three with the new UK variant, and 11 deaths overall we head into lockdown, or a period of national pause as she likes to call it, for two weeks from 3 February. Air travel to and from the island will be reduced and all inbound travellers will take an antigen test on arrival in addition to the present protocols.

Bars, restaurants, and gyms will close. Supermarkets and essential shops will remain open between 8.00am and 3pm. There will be a curfew in place between 7pm and 6am. We should remain at home unless shopping or taking our daily exercise. There was no mention of beaches or golf courses being off limits; something for me to find out.

So, we intend to maximise the time we have till 3 February to get out and about.

Over the past couple of days, we have visited two more beaches on the south coast. We go in the afternoon to avoid the midday sun and stay until the sun sets. It is always a wonder to watch the sun setting into the sea, sipping a cold beer and marvel at the relative tranquillity of the beautiful beaches framed by swaying palm trees and glorious colours in the sky.

I also don't know of many places in the world where you can drive your car up to the edge of the beach, park under the branches of a bearded fig or Baobab tree and walk straight onto the sand and relax on a lounger.

Most beaches have a good bar/restaurant and Rockley beach is no exception with an early happy hour. We enjoyed a late lunch of fish, salad and chicken satay, the best I have ever tasted outside of Asia, before a swim, exploration of the underwater coral and drying off in the late afternoon sun; a perfect way to end a day.

1 February 2020

Sugar, sugar

Sugar Sugar, no, I am not talking about the big hit song of 1970 by the Archies - (how many of us remember that?) – but the real sugar that grows here in Barbados. We are surrounded by fields of sugar cane that border the local roads and tracks; a pleasant feature of the landscape as the tall perennial cane grasses sway gently in the wind.

Sugar cane is familiar to me as I grew up in Assam, India, where large fields of it were grown on our tea plantation. As children, my brother and I used to sneak in amongst the tall canes and chop off stalks to chew, to get at the sweet juice within and spitting out the fibrous remains afterwards; pure heaven for kids who had no access to confectionery or sweets.

In the 17th century British and European planters took advantage of the ideal growing conditions to introduce, plant, grow and harvest sugar cane. By mid-century Barbados was an economic powerhouse built on sugar and one of the most valuable colonies in the British Empire. The planters of the time became fabulously wealthy and the plantation homes that remain are a testament to this and the architecture of the time. Many still remain and some are now a tourist attraction.

Halton Great House, just down the road from where we are staying, is one such plantation house built around 1660. It is one of the oldest on the island and was established by one Thomas Rous of a prominent Quaker family. Its present owners have restored it to its former glory and modernised it to provide a venue for weddings and corporate entertainment.

The fortunes of the planters, however, eventually declined with the advent of sugar beet that could be planted and grown on European and American soil.

With the introduction of sugar came an influx of black African slave labour taking the place of indentured and press-ganged white workers who up to this point had been used to farm the land. The balance of ethnicity on the island also gradually changed from being predominantly white to predominantly black. The one unifying feature was the language spoken which was English as different African tribal dialects faded away. Today, the official language is English but the colloquial language is Bajan, an English-based creole dialect.

Myth or reality? I grew up believing sugar derived from sugar cane was healthier than refined white sugar from sugar beet. Alas, this is a myth. Both forms of sugar are high in Sucrose with the minimal balance formed of impurities. The effects of too much sugar in our diet are now well known with increasing rates of obesity across the World. As with all things moderation in consumption is the key. However, I am still looking to sneak into a local cane field and cut off a stalk to chew.

3 February 2021

Reflections

It's been a month since we arrived in Barbados on the 2nd of January. To celebrate we dined out at a very smart place called Primo; modern, well designed and situated with the sea swirling by the dining deck. You could be forgiven for thinking that you were dining on board a large boat. Most of Barbados appeared to be dining out, too, as it was the last evening before our local two-week lock down and the place was packed with the smart set as well visitors like us. So, service was slow but this gave us ample time to sip our Margaritas and reflect on the past month.

Apart from the wonderful beaches, sunsets, the wild east coast, plantation homes, sea views, half-finished houses surrounded by automobiles in varying stages of deterioration and the cultivated countryside we have met some interesting characters.

On the beach yesterday this tall, slim, good looking black guy with hair in braids came up to us.

'How are yawl? I'm known as the doctor. Anything you want that's good for you I can get.'

'We are in good health,' I replied, 'so no thanks.' The penny then dropped.

The good 'doctor' was offering certain substances to 'uplift' one's spirits. Thankfully, substances of the kind he was offering have never been a vice of ours so he went away empty handed.

Then, we went into a local hotel bar above the beach which was empty apart from one black guy standing by the bar doing something with a glass. Needing a beer, I addressed him and asked for a beer, not spotting the expensive loafers and the gold watch on his wrist.

'I don't work here, I am a guest in the hotel,' came the reply in a beautifully spoken cut glass English accent straight out of the West End.

It turns out he is an art dealer dealing in high end impressionist art with a handful of selected clients. His uncle is a high court judge on the island and he is relocating his operation from Chelsea to Bridgetown.

Over the next half an hour he gave us a fascinating insight into the art world and some big deals, he had stitched together. He then asked if I would like to invest in some high-end art. As a pensioner of limited means, I politely declined!

Then there's the golf club, which like clubs all over the world, contains a recognisable set of characters - the comedian, the raconteur, the introspective, the drinker, the golf nerd; a mix of locals, long stay Brits, Irish, Scots, Canadians escaping the winter and Welcome Stampers like us. Golfers are a friendly bunch and we have been invited to join various parties for drinks following a round but with Covid prevalent have made the decision to avoid closer contact at this stage.

So, we are now confined to our ground floor apartment. But with the sun shining, a pleasant breeze, a verandah to enjoy and access to a large garden that contains many mature trees and shrubs we will make the most of the next two weeks here watching the antics of the chickens, goats and ducks that roam at will. Of course, we are permitted to visit the local supermarket for supplies so we will not be totally incommunicado.

5 February 2021

It's a Rum business

I have already mentioned sugar but I can't talk about sugar without mentioning rum!

Sitting in a beach bar one afternoon we watched as three tall, frosted, glasses of an exotic looking tall pink cocktail was served to a party at a nearby table.

'What is that?' I asked the bar attendant.

'Strawberry Daiquiri,' came the reply.

'We'll have to try one of those,' I responded. 'What is it made of?' I asked, not being an aficionado of cocktails.

'It's rum based, as many of our cocktails are,' he said.

'Right, we'll have two,' I replied.

It was a pleasant drink but like the rum punch we had

tried on a previous occasion a bit sweet for both of us. I think I'll stick to wine and beer, my normal staples, though I am partial to a Margarita.

Rum is a major export of Barbados and the rum producers would argue that the best rum comes from Barbados. The world's oldest known distillery is Mount Gay, situated here, which began production in 1703.

However, rum was produced long before this as the juice of the canes and molasses proved ideal materials for its production. Then it was known as 'Kill-devil' or 'Rumbullion' before it became commonly known as rum.

By 1655, the British Navy had begun giving a half pint of Rum to each sailor daily which, mixed with lime, was seen as the antidote to scurvy which killed more sailors than naval military action.

Popular modern cocktails that include Rum are Daiquiri, Pina Colada, Mojito, Mai Tai, Cuba Libre and Zombie! But then you cocktail drinkers know all this.

However, a visit to a local Rum producer is now on our list of things to do once our two-week lock down is over.

10 February 2021

Bath beach and exercise

Today completes week one of our local two-week lock down.

We dragged ourselves out of bed at 5.45am to ensure we left promptly at 6.00am to get to a new beach we hadn't visited before. We wanted to catch the sunrise and maximise our narrow three-hour window of allowable exercise time; 6.00 to 9.00am.

Bath beach is, apparently, one of the safest beaches on the east coast of the island and unlike several other bays on this coast, there are rarely strong currents. This is because there is a coral reef barrier some way offshore which creates a lagoon like effect.

There are also the remains of an old railway line that once

ran from Bridgetown to Bellepaine, further up the coast, with a station at Bath Beach. The completed line to Belleplaine was officially inaugurated in 1883 and, initially, was a commercial success as the cars carried sugar, freight and passengers. But with declining levels of freight and passengers and a lack of proper, ongoing, re-investment the railway system deteriorated and was discontinued in 1937 with the rails lifted and scrapped the following year.

We arrived at the beach, parked up and wandered through the attractive Casuarina trees down onto the sand smelling the sea spray on the slight breeze. The sea was indeed calm and we plunged in up to our waists. The water felt delightfully warm to our touch.

Apparently, the sea temperature here is an average of 27 degrees in February. I thought back to my last swim in the sea off Eastbourne the previous summer when the temperature was 17 degrees. Today, it's showing as 8 degrees!

We watched as two men with snorkels, and what appeared to be spear guns, waded right out to the edge of the reef and began snorkelling along its length.

'Let's walk further out,' I said, very soon regretting my suggestion as our feet began to encounter a sharp, rocky sea bed. It was impossible to leave the immediate sandy underwater strip along the edge of the beach without damaging our feet. Plastic sandals or rubber beach shoes are what we need for this I thought.

So, we confined ourselves to the shore line, immersing ourselves in the sea before walking along the length of the beach.

The east coast beach areas are sparsely populated compared to the west but we saw some pretty-looking wooden chalets tucked in amongst the trees just above the shoreline.

After a couple of hours, we left to drive home for a well-earned breakfast. The route back took us past an impressive, stately looking eighteenth century stone-built mansion with a palm tree lined drive. We turned in for a look. The estate we entered is the home of Codrington College, the oldest theological college in the western hemisphere and the oldest tertiary education institution in the region.

It was founded in 1745 after Christopher Codrington, a wealthy sugar cane planter and former Governor General, had bequeathed the estate and considerable money at his death in 1710.

The setting of the college is impressive with its lily pond, driveway lined with tall Cabbage Palm trees and its situation on a hilltop overlooking the Atlantic Ocean.

We made it back by 9.00am and the end of our exercise period with minutes to spare.

14 February 2021

Barbados or bust

Being a petrol-head (I worked in Formula 1 many years ago, but that's another story) I was interested to see the types of cars here and whether I could pick up an American or British sporting classic for a reasonable price. No chance! Cars are a valuable commodity in Barbados and command premium prices even for something quite pedestrian and ancient.

Being a former British colony and a member of the Commonwealth where the Queen is still Head of State, I had expected to see some British cars; but I have yet to spot one. No older American cars either.

I know there is classic and vintage car scene here but there has been no sign of their cars on the road or at a show but I guess Covid has put paid to that for the moment.

As I have commented before almost all the cars are Japanese and the majority are over 15 years old. So, maybe I would spot a historic Japanese sports car like a Datsun 240/260/280 Z or the more modern Mazda MX5 (Miata) convertible. I haven't spotted a single Japanese sports car either. They are all saloons though I have seen sport versions of the Subaru, Honda and Mitsubishi on the roads.

And they keep them running long past their sell by date. Many have exotic colour schemes and are clearly cherished.

When they finally do fall off the road they are kept at home as decaying wrecks gradually being stripped of usable parts. Many just lie abandoned in the countryside with vegetation invading their interiors. Maybe the government should introduce a scrappage scheme to rid the landscape of this blight. Maybe they have; something I need to check.

It's not completely a Japanese scene however. There are Korean makes here and older and more modern BMWs and Mercedes, but a handful by comparison.

Apart from a handful of highways in and around Bridgetown the roads severely test the tyres and suspension of cars. Frequent patching up of potholes and deteriorating tarmac make for a bone jarring ride most of the time. I am amazed at how well our 15-year-old Suzuki Swift rental with 228,000 kilometres on the clock handles them.

The driving infrastructure is a mix of English and European. They drive on the left like the UK but speed limits and speedos are designated in kilometres like Europe and you buy gasoline in litres.

I had thought to import my BMW 2.5 series 3 sports convertible here but cars have to be under four years old, or over 20 years old and qualify for classic status. My BMW falls in the middle of these categories. So, I will be driving a Japanese saloon for the rest of our stay.

22 February 2021

Curfew

Three days ago, with rising numbers of Covid cases and deaths, the government announced a weekend curfew. Apart from key workers the population is to be confined to their homes and no cars are allowed on the roads. Supermarkets and food outlets would, as normal under the present lock down, be closed over the weekend.

We had planned to move to a new apartment over the weekend so had to readjust our plans and ensure we were in situ at the new place by 7pm on Friday evening. We gave up on the large house we had originally decided upon wishing to stay on the more deserted east side of the island.

Our new abode is near the Ragged Point light house on the Atlantic coast. It's much quieter here and we can see and hear the sea. The light house is also visible on the cliff top nearby.

The locale is more urban so there are no goats, chickens and ducks running around and no barking dogs either. There are also no mosquitoes. At the previous property we bore our daily bites with increasing stoicism but it's a relief not to have to spray our exposed limbs with 'Jungle Juice', 'Go' or one of any number of other propriety products that are meant to repel the little blood suckers.

We do have a house guest though, a green lizard (Anolis Extremus), which, unlike the mice in our house in England which gnaw at everything, appears harmless.

Today is Monday so we are free of the weekend curfew but the Health Minister, a Lieutenant Colonel Bostic, is not a happy bunny as over the weekend the mainly asymptomatic younger generation were still out on the streets, hanging out then returning home where maybe three generations of the family live and so passing on the virus to their elderly relatives.

There was a great comment on a local news site: 'When Bostic locked down the weekend that was a superb move. He snared all those barbers, beauticians, home bakers, hair dressers, nail techs, artisans, gardeners, car washers and home delivery persons selling everything from weed to sex. They could not go on the road. Bostic should clamp down like that each weekend and he will reap real good rewards in this fight. Go ahead Lt. Col you seem to know who is disobeying and spreading Covid.'

We are still in lock down so everyone should still be at home but under the guise of visiting the supermarket I think independent business people have been carrying on as normal. But it was a relief to get out between 6 and 9am to go for a long walk along the cliff top.

Unusually, we had a very overcast and still day yesterday which lasted all day. Like a grey UK winter's day though warm.

It turns out it was a plume of sand from the Sahara that had blown across the Atlantic and sat over us until the breeze freshened over-night and dispersed it westwards. Amazing how that sand can reach the UK and the Caribbean.

1 March 2021

Lockdown eases

Today, we emerged from lock down but only partially. An additional exercise period has been granted from between 3 and 6 in the afternoon. Supermarkets can open on Saturdays, all mini-marts can open along with a variety of other outdoor oriented businesses. Hair dressers, barbers, nail shops and the like have to remain closed.

With the overcast weather of the past few days giving way to sunshine we revisited Rockley Beach on the south coast, one of our favourites. It was good to back on the beach and in the sea at a time of day that suits us.

Over the weekend we spotted a fantastic looking large caterpillar on the tree outside our verandah munching away at a leaf. The tree in question is a Frangipani tree and these caterpillars are, apparently, Frangipani worms and can grow to six inches plus. Two of them can strip a Frangipani tree in a couple of days and as the leaves are poisonous, they are left alone by other predators, their flashy colour scheme acting as a warning that to eat me would be a dangerous business. Maybe they turn into attractive butterflies? Apparently not, they turn into big grey moths with a six-inch wingspan.

Then yesterday morning I heard a bird I had never heard before. It sounded a bit like a crow but was clearly coming from a big bird. I walked outside to take a look, to see a huge monkey jump from the roof onto the wall beside me. It was the monkey making that noise; not a familiar sound. Luckily, it ran off. We must keep the mesh framed verandah screens closed when inside as it would be very easy for one to come in and steal anything from a banana to a pair of sunglasses.

So, this is turning into a regular botanical experience here.

7 March 2021

Living like a Lord

'Get aloft and put another reef in the mainsail,' the captain shouted as a huge wave swept over the port side of the Portuguese carrack.

'We need to fine Bridgetown soon Captain, the men can barely keep pace pumping out the water from the hold,' reported his mate.

The winds had gradually increased in intensity during the evening and the ship was wallowing badly in the heavy sea not helped by their full load of cargo.

'Lights captain, on the starboard bow,' shouted a lookout.

The captain peered through the spray and the darkness and could just make out several pinpoints of light that extended upwards into the dark skies.

'That has to be Bridgetown,' he murmured to himself. He made a decision.

'Ten points to starboard,' he shouted to the helmsman, who turned the wheel.

'See those lights sailor, keep the ship headed towards them.'

'Aye aye, sir.'

The carrack lurched towards the shore. Moments later

there was a loud rending crack and the ship shuddered to a halt as if some invisible force had gripped the vessel.

'Reef, we've struck a...,' a voice shouted suddenly cut off amid the vicious winds that howled over the stricken ship.

The masts snapped under the impact and a great weight of sail and wood fell onto the vessel and into the raging sea alongside. Men were tossed overboard as if they were feathers and those that were clinging to rigging and ship's woodwork were swamped by huge waves that rolled relentlessly over the side of the carrack. The ship and its crew were doomed.

In the wolf light of dawn several hard looking, bearded men set off from the shore towards the wreck of what had once been a fine ship. They hadn't come to rescue the vessel or its occupants but to plunder it of its valuable cargo.

It was December 1834 and the ship was one of several that had been lured onto the treacherous reefs along this part of the Barbados coast tricked by lanterns hung in the trees extending along and up from the shoreline.

Legend has it that this was the work of Samuel Lord Hall whose beautiful Georgian castellated mansion and estates extended across the land along the cliffs above the shore.

Sam Lord was an intelligent, charismatic, ruthlessly ambitious businessman and buccaneer. It is believed that

much of his wealth derived from the spoils of ships lured onto the reefs below his estate. Apparently, there was a tunnel to the shore that led down from the house and the booty including much gold and silver was secreted in underground cells dug out of the rock.

The beautiful house was completed in 1820 and was unique among the fine homes on the island at the time. It was furnished with the latest fabrics, paintings and furniture of the period as well as antiques. There were massive regency mirrors, exquisite mahogany furniture and Italian, Dutch, French and English masterpieces; much of it said to originate from the wrecked ships or the from the proceeds of sale. The verandahs were constructed of marble and an extensive formal garden laid out.

The house became known as Sam Lord's Castle and was Sam's base though he spent many years in Britain. Sam died in 1844 and his estate passed to his children.

As the nineteenth century gave way to the twentieth the estate was sold and had several owners including an English insurance magnate who spent almost £1 million pounds on restoration during the 1940s. Guests included Queen Elizabeth and Prince Phillip.

It was eventually acquired by the Marriot hotel group in 1972 who transformed it into a beautiful destination hotel. Marriot eventually divested itself of the property but its future owners were unable to invest in its upkeep as a prestigious hotel and it fell into disrepair and neglect with a fire sealing its fate in October 2010.

The 'castle' and grounds have now been acquired by the Wyndham Resort group financed by the Export Import Bank of China and their plans include restoration of the house and transforming the estate into 450 room resort.

We visited the ruins yesterday and they are a sad sight. The once gracious house is gradually decaying and the gardens are overgrown. The public still have access, though the main construction site is sealed off.

Walking through the grounds and beach area one can still see traces of marble balustrades and formal pathways. Marriot's beach bar and leisure area are covered in creepers and detritus from locals who come for barbeques and beach parties. The beach is unkempt and clifftop walkways and steps have crumbled away. It's a depressing vision but hopefully the Wyndham group will restore it to its former glory.

As you stand on the beach and look out towards the reefs one can imagine those poor souls ending their lives as their ships were lured to destruction for unscrupulous gain. Whether Sam the Man was to blame, or other local pirates, who utilised the natural terrain his estate afforded while he was overseas, will always remain the subject of conjecture.

18 March 2021

Restrictions, ruins, rum and drug runners

Lock down here eased last Monday, the 15th of March. Curfew slips back to 9.00pm to 6.00am and restaurants can reopen as can most businesses except gyms, pleasure craft, team sports and individual sports like squash. But hiking and golf are possible! One cannot congregate around bars and exercise times continue to be limited to 6.00-9.00am and 3.00-6.00pm. It's bit of a mish mash as golf is permissible all day as is hiking but exercise periods remain the same. Seems odd. But I am pleased to able to get back to golf.

We took the opportunity to visit another location like Sam Lord's Castle.

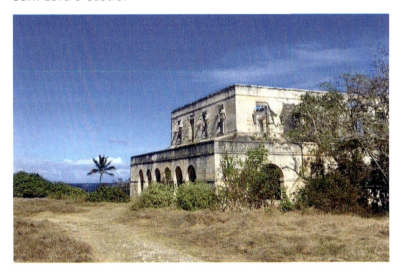

Perched on the cliff-top, above another lovely isolated beach, is the ruin of a grand house known as Harrismith

Great House. Apparently, it's not as old as other plantation mansions having been built in the 1920s from cut coral stone by a Roland Henry Taylor, a planter from Wakefield in the parish of St John. A local told me that it had been used as a seaside house and may have been a hotel.

Its name appears to originate from a namesake town in South Africa founded in 1849 and named after the British Governor there, Sir Harry Smith.

Lieutenant-General Sir Henry George Wakelyn Smith, 1st Baronet, GCB (1787 - 1860) was a heroic soldier and military commander in the mould of Wellington who regarded him highly. He served across the British empire from America to the Napoleonic Wars, India and South Africa. His enduring love affair and marriage to a young Spanish noblewoman was the subject of a novel by Georgette Heyer. But quite what the connection between the name of the house in Barbados and Harrismith in South Africa or the man himself is unclear.

We ventured down to the beach and walked its length. For the first time we spotted jellyfish including one remarkable looking blue one which could be either a blue striped jellyfish or a Portuguese Man O' War. That decided it for me in terms of going in the water, though the sea was rough and the undertow looked vicious.

Also embedded in the sand along the high tide mark was an abandoned skiff or motor boat. It had powerful looking twin outboard motors and was a low-slung sleek craft. It reminded me of the vessels' smugglers used between China and Hong Kong and I can imagine its use here was for some nefarious activity, possibly involving drugs.

After all this excitement we repaired to a restaurant in St Lawrence Gap to enjoy something different to my cooking. The name of the establishment was Castaways, a fitting title after our visit to Harrismith's 'smugglers cove'.

8 April 2021

Gardener's world

Despite life being almost back to normal we tend to follow the government's advice which is to stay at home as much as possible. Neither of us have had the Covid jab yet though will do so when available.

Being at home our attention has turned to the garden that comes with our apartment.

in the UK I was quite a keen gardener and knew most of the local flowers, shrubs and trees. Out here it's completely different. Most I don't recognise. What I need, I thought to myself, is an app that recognises leaves and flowers and tells you what they are. I finally found a free one last night and downloaded it. Called Plant Net it's excellent. I have had great fun over the past two days walking around the garden identifying the various trees, shrubs and flowers.

One morning we discovered our wonderful sweet smelling Frangipani tree, a Pulmeria Obtusa, covered in at least fifty of the colourful Frangipani worms munching away at the leaves. Fortunately, they were quite small so we managed to get them off the tree.

Whether it's due to the Spring and the slight increase in temperature but we have also noticed an increase in mongooses and rats. Some bright spark two hundred years ago thought they would import mongooses from India to control the rat population.

Unfortunately, mongooses operate during the day and sleep at night while rats come out at night so that was no good. And now we have too many mongooses. They did eat all the snakes though. So, the farmers now have three pests to deal with – rats, mongooses and monkeys – which are all partial to sugar cane and other crops.

Then this evening in the garden we noticed a brightly marked shell, about the size of a golf ball, moving. On closer examination it was being propelled along by its occupant, a crab like being. A quick search on Google reveals that this may be a hermit crab. Hermit crabs are crustaceans. Crustaceans, apparently, are a class of creatures with segmented bodies with external skeletons. They can live either on land or in water. They're not true crabs, though. With an exposed body they protect themselves by searching for abandoned shells, usually sea snail shells, of which there are plenty inland. When they find one that fits, they tuck themselves inside it for protection and carry it with them wherever they go.

After our labours we decided to decamp to the beach yesterday for a swim but the sea which is normally a clear aquamarine blue was a dirty green. It was full of small particles of sea weed known as Sargassum; not pleasant to swim in. We are guessing that this phenomenon is also a result of a rise in temperatures. We are hoping it's a temporary situation.

10 April 2021

Ash alert

We woke up this morning to a very dark and gloomy day. I'm in the UK, I thought only half awake, and what is that whitish covering on the trees outside, a light dusting of snow? But, of course, we are not in the UK but in sunny, balmy Barbados. What's going on?

I took a look outside in the half-light to see everything coated in a light grey powder. Sand from the Sahara? But it's too grey for that. I fired up the laptop and read that La Soufriere volcano on St Vincent, an island one hundred miles to the west of us, had erupted three times the previous evening sending an ash cloud up 51,000 feet. Barbados was now feeling the fallout from this.

There was a smell of burning in the air which stung the eyes and caught in the back of the throat. Thank goodness for our Covid masks which we immediately put on.

Our landlord advised us to close all our windows and doors, switch our fans on and stay inside with the message that it should be clearer tomorrow.

That's okay with us, I thought, as the Masters golf tournament in Augusta in the US was on TV and we could watch that. However, a short while ago play was suspended as a weather front with lightning began to move through that part of Georgia. I'm wondering if that is also related to the erupting volcano on St Vincent.

It's only 4.30 in the afternoon but maybe it's time to have a beer and watch something else or read until play resumes. Justin Rose, an Englishman, leads the tournament and I'm hoping he will finally prevail having had one arm in the green jacket three years ago in 2017. He narrowly lost in a play-off to Sergio Garcia.

16 April 2021

'Death at Ragged Point'

One week after the volcanic eruptions in St Vincent the ash has finally ceased to fall regularly on Barbados. It's been a grim week; of course, not so grim as for the poor folks on St Vincent where the volcano continues to spew forth lava and ash. The ash has achieved what Covid restrictions didn't, namely keeping everyone off the streets and inside and wearing masks when outside.

Monday the 12th of April marked the beginning of a national clean-up of the island, not for the ash but of the island in general. I have already mentioned the profusion of car wrecks littering the island along with all other kinds of domestic and industrial detritus.

Barbados is a paradise when on the beaches and in the gardens and in the northern rural interior but is blighted elsewhere. Back in March the prime minister commented that she wanted to see a considerably cleaner Barbados by May Day 2021. She made her feelings known about the untidy state of the country. She said there was a time when residents did not hesitate to clean up neighbouring properties, recognising that while the neighbour 'may be living in foreign, the rats are living at me'.

The timing of the ash fall across the island was unfortunate though prescient as locals turned out in their thousands with brooms, shovels and hoses to clean up the centimetres thick dust and begin to evaluate what else needed to be done.

The roads look like they have been coated with smooth cement, filling in and masking the potholes. That's useful but no doubt traffic and rain will remove the layer. Meanwhile, its slippery stuff to drive on. We did venture out to our local beach today to see the effects there. Instead of a sparkling white, pink beach, the sand was covered in a layer of grey ash except between the high and low tide marks. The sea looked grey as well. The palm trees and normally verdant undergrowth were a dirty grey. Hopefully, the rains will clean all this away before holiday makers once again return to the island.

With the onset of the ash blizzard, we closed all windows

and doors, switched our fans on and remained inside during the five days since. Once the Masters golf tournament in Atlanta concluded on the Sunday, Antonina suggested I write a murder mystery during our incarceration maybe involving the geo-climatic conditions we were suffering. I couldn't quite run to that but have written and published a short murder mystery titled 'Death at Ragged Point'. Amazing what can be achieved be in a week. Here's the summary:

'Sir Peter Carter, a British billionaire industrialist, is found dead at his Barbados residence. Dying of cancer this was not unexpected. Given his prominence the Commissioner of Police wants to be sure he died of natural causes. DCI Wayne Johnson is tasked to investigate. He discovers that Sir Peter was murdered but uncovering the motive and proving who killed him taxes all his skills. His investigation leads him into the Colombian drug world, international money laundering and family conflicts.'

Hooked? Keen to find out who dunnit? The book can be found on Amazon along with several others I have written since.

18 April 2021

Covid jab Bajan style

'There's a Polyclinic (medical centre) out at Six Roads, opposite the supermarket. You could have a chat with them,' my neighbour said.

'Great! Thanks,' I replied, 'I haven't heard anything from my enquiries via the government Covid website or from their WhatsApp numbers.'

'Well, try there.'

We are keen to have the Covid vaccine particularly me at my age! And the PM has said the jab in Barbados would be available for all including visitors but, so far, I have had no luck with responses to my enquiries to the various government contact details published exhorting those on the island to apply for a Covid inoculation. I had already resigned myself to waiting until I was back in the UK.

But nothing ventured, nothing gained and as we needed a couple of things from the supermarket, mainly wine and some beers, we took a drive out to Six Roads. Maybe, we could find out at the Polyclinic how to get on a list.

Unfortunately, the supermarket was closed but the Polyclinic looked open and not that busy. We parked up and found the entrance where a small queue of eight people had formed.

'Is this the queue for Reception?' I asked.

'No man, this is for the vaccine,' came the reply from an elderly male local.

Before we could decide what to do a brisk looking nurse with bright orange toe nails and clip board in hand marched out and counted us up.

'Great, ten. Come with me all of you,' she commanded.

We followed her inside and were assigned a group of chairs.

'Do you think these people have appointments,' I whispered to Antonina. 'I thought walk-ins were discouraged.'

'Let's see,' she replied.

The brisk looking nurse asked for our details which she entered onto a blue card. Fortunately, we had our passports with us; mandatory for all non-residents. It appeared that we would be vaccinated today; no getting on a list or appointment needed. And so began a chaotic hour and half as we were shovelled from one holding area to another before taking seats stretching down a long narrow corridor.

There was a creative poster on the wall that caught my attention.

Then the cabaret started.

A nurse pulling a trolley helped by a male assistant, sashayed down the corridor beside us, singing a reggae number and moving her hips in time to the rhythm, as she whipped out syringe after syringe and plunged them into our waiting arms. Each penetration of the flesh was accompanied by a loud shriek, as if in pain, followed by a peal of laughter. She was certainly enjoying her work. It was terrifying but entertaining.

After a 15-minute wait to ensure no-one passed out, or went blue, our batch of ten were handed a blue card each and discharged.

The whole experience was so surreal I still can't quite believe I've had the Covid vaccine, AstraZeneca, here and for free. God bless the PM, Mia Mottley. We go back in June for the booster.

'I now need a drink' I thought to myself. But, alas, nurse said no alcohol for two days!

20 April 2021

'Cannon to right of them, Cannon to left of them'

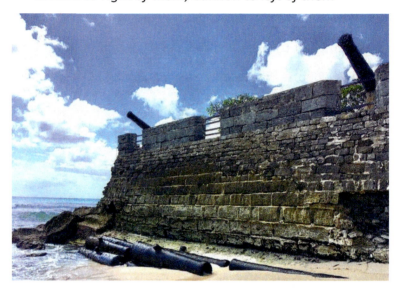

Many of you will recognise these words from the poem 'The Charge of the Light Brigade' by Alfred Lord Tennyson.

Cannons form a part of Barbados's historical legacy; more of which in a moment.

At first hand, we saw the impact of Covid on the hotel business in Barbados. We visited the Hilton Hotel as Antonina had booked a hair appointment with a stylist based in the hotel complex. Situated on Needham's Point its position is enviable as it is surrounded by open sea on three sides with access to three pretty beaches. No other hotels share this space. It occupies a unique position on the island.

During our day there we counted five hotel guests. The

complex was deserted apart from staff who were busy cleaning up the ash from the volcanic eruption on St Vincent some twelve days ago. The Hilton, along with all the hotels in Barbados, must be bleeding badly financially.

The beach, normally full of blue sunbeds and parasols, was deserted.

The position of the hotel is not only enviable because of its scenic location. It is of historical significance. Somehow, in 1966, Conrad Hilton managed to build a hotel on land which houses Charles Fort (formerly Needham's Fort) and the Needham's Point lighthouse, the second oldest lighthouse in Barbados built in 1855. The hotel is now located within Barbados' sole UNESCO World Heritage site, Historic Bridgetown and its Garrison.

Needham's Fort was constructed in the early 17th century. In 1649, the King of England, Charles I, was beheaded and the government was taken over by Oliver Cromwell. Barbados remained loyal to the royalists, and in 1660 when King Charles II was restored to the throne, the fort's name was changed to Charles Fort.

By the late 17th century, Charles Fort had become the most powerful of the coastal defence structures on Barbados with some 36 cannons at its disposal. It guarded the entrance to Carlyle Bay and Bridgetown, the main port and city on the island. Additional fortifications and cannons were added in the mid-18th century. Britain was at war with both Spain and France, and Barbados, apart from its ideal geographical military location in the western hemisphere, was an economic powerhouse based on sugar that needed protection.

The Light Brigade faced around 50 Russian artillery pieces in the Battle of Balaclava. French or Spanish warships attempting to storm Bridgetown would face an equal number if not more cannon.

An astonishing amount of cannon were placed on Barbados at key access points to the island. To date more than 400 have been unearthed buried in the sand, hidden under rubble and lying in long abandoned stone embrasures around the coast line. More than half the cannon were cast in the 17th century in England. The oldest cannon found was cast in 1620 and many are rare. One cannon is so rare that the only other existing example lies in the Tower of London.

Standing on the ramparts of Charles Fort surrounded by stonework and cannons you gaze out over an empty azure sea. One can imagine a squaddie of the period looking out for the topsails of frigates and galleons determining whether they were friendly or hostile.

The remains of the fort now form part of the gardens of

the Hilton hotel and are occasionally used for parties and functions. I cannot think of a more striking setting as the sun goes down over the Caribbean Sea and the remaining cannon are silhouetted against the setting sun.

4 May 2021

Island Life

One of my oldest friends has asked whether I would describe day-to-day living, shopping, interactions with neighbours and so forth which seems a pertinent thing to do.

We live in a middle-class neighbourhood. Despite that even the more affluent locals seem to like living in houses that are unfinished. Many lack an outer coating of paint which, with weathering, makes them appear derelict on first appearance.

I believe this is a tax dodge as one pays a certain amount of tax on a completed house ie painted. Unpainted houses are deemed unfinished.

Establishing a garden does not appear to be of much

interest either. Many big houses sit in isolated plots of scrubland which only adds to the appearance of dereliction. And architecturally, house design here for the more affluent is a mess; a mix of Renaissance, Baroque, Neo-classical and Art noveau. Earlier houses are influenced by Jacobean design elements and in many parts of the island, where there are older plantation houses, you could be forgiven for thinking you were driving through the French countryside.

My immediate neighbour, an attractive mid-fifties lady, runs a car rental business. Hers is an interesting background. She's of Guyanese descent, married a Frenchman and lived for many years on the Ivory coast, Africa, before settling in London. She speaks with a strong South London accent. She came to Barbados fifteen years ago, bought a plot of land and built a house.

One of her closest friends, a local, lives in a large house overlooking the cliffs nearby and dabbles in property development. On her land is a popular restaurant that the chef and his partner lease from her.

The owners of the green house directly opposite live in the UK and have not visited their home here since Covid struck back in 2020. Many houses on our estate appear empty.

Another neighbour is a magistrate and has a beautiful small house that overlooks the sea.

Bajans are a friendly, courteous people who greet you in a traditional British way. No Hi or G'day, It's good morning, good afternoon and good evening. They wave when you drive by and will always greet you.

Given Covid and its restrictions we have not been as neighbourly as we might usually be so haven't got to know many local people. This is compounded by living in the Parish of St Philip on the east coast, a semi-rural environment which suits us. There are no cases of Covid out here compared to the built-up areas of the capital Bridgetown and the south west and west coast communities.

The island is small, some twenty miles north to south by fifteen miles east to west. This means that one can easily reach the more popular areas and the capital's shops. Having said that, catch the rush hour and one can be stuck for over half an hour crawling along the roads in heavy traffic.

By choice, we have avoided the capital and more built-up urban areas and fortunately, a modern shopping complex, reminiscent of those found in American towns, lies in an isolated location only six miles away. Called Six Roads it contains one of the largest and best equipped supermarkets on the island, two banks, a post office, gas station, Polyclinic (medical surgery), Courts, a home retail store, Chefette (think McDonalds), clothes shops and a variety of smaller retail outlets. So, we have almost everything we need on our doorstep.

In terms of the cost of living, one can live here more cheaply than in the UK in terms of property rental payments and utilities. Fuel is about the same. The kicker is food. Being an island almost everything has to be flown in. Our supermarket bills can be up to double that in the UK. Okay, we don't need to eat Yeo Valley probiotic yoghurt, an English west country firm whose products we delightedly found on the shelves of the supermarket. A 1kg carton costs GBP8.69, considerably more than in the UK. Said supermarket must also have a tie-up with Tesco as many of their own label products are stocked. I have discovered that in the heat here Tesco baked beans, once opened, survive much longer in the fridge than Heinz's. I hate to think what preservatives they use.

Products are not always available. For example, there have been no cloves of garlic for sale for some six weeks. Then they appeared on the shelves as flights resumed to Barbados following the volcanic eruption on neighbouring St Vincent.

We determined to source our fruit and veg from local sources, mainly stalls along the roadside out in the country, but found the savings not to be that great, just a few dollars.

Alcohol is generally expensive. A bottle of Yellow Tail Shiraz from Australia costs about GBP7.00 in the UK and that would be a budget wine there. Here it is a premium brand costing around GBP11.50. The cheaper wines from the Caribbean and South America are frankly disgusting.

Rum, the staple alcoholic drink of the island is cheap, but

I have never liked the stuff, unfortunately.

A six pack of local beer comes out at around GBP4.85 which is okay.

Being British I drink a lot of tea and a pack of 50 Lipton's Yellow Label teabags comes out at GBP3.00 while an 11oz pack of Arabica ground coffee is GBP8.74.

Meat and fish are more expensive though local fish bought
at a fish market would be cheaper.

Try as we might it's hard to reduce our food and drinks bills. I'm not ready to become an ascetic or give up alcohol.

How do the locals manage we thought to ourselves? A quick Google search shows that average wages between the UK and Barbados are broadly similar. Maybe the locals exist much more on the local staples of bread fruit, plantains, yams, mangoes and coconuts and locally sourced fish and chicken and eschew Yeo Valley probiotic yoghurt!

Apart from the cost one has to get used to queuing in the supermarkets. This isn't down to Covid though that doesn't help. I believe things could be organised more efficiently but the Bajans are a patient people and don't seem to mind queuing. They have a relaxed attitude to life.

In terms of daily life, we exist in minimal amounts of clothing going barefoot inside and flip flops outside. One can save a small fortune in clothing bills. Every day the temperature is the same, between 26-28C. The humidity is around 70%. At night it's around 24C. I've forgotten what it's like to wear trousers, pullovers, coats and so forth. The heat is not of the crippling variety. Okay, you don't want to be working outside in the mid-day sun but it's bearable and a lovely temperature at the beginning and end of a day. We love the climate here and feel much healthier than in the UK.

The constant humidity, however, means rust is an ever-present problem for anything metallic; not dissimilar to the UK.

Golf, now that is a problem. By that, I mean sourcing things like golf shoes, gloves and clubs. There doesn't appear to be a good golf shop on the island. Next time I'm back in the UK I will bring back some shoes and extra gloves. I guess given the small population, and the fact it's a minority sport, it's probably not worth a major retailer's time setting up here.

We have established a daily routine. Three times a week we play golf and visit a beach to walk and swim. Often, we'll stop for a drink and dinner in a beachside restaurant, watching the sun dip into the Caribbean Sea. A couple of times a week we go food shopping. We also take excursions to see the sights and will do more of this as Covid restrictions have eased.

Otherwise, we read, I write and we spend time in the garden where we have propagated a number of plants. We take a daily walk along the cliff tops and have our main meal in the evenings with a glass of wine. We then sit out on the verandah gazing at the stars, breathing in the smell of the Frangipani and other scents on the night air. Evenings are wonderful here. Sometimes we catch a movie on Netflix. It's a very relaxing existence.

Speaking of which, it's time for our evening cocktail!

4 May 2021

Hunte's Gardens, a tropical paradise

As one drives across the island numerous signs appear pointing the way to Hunte's Gardens. Today we resolved to find these gardens, see if they were open and check them out. They were open, we met the man himself, paid the entrance fee and entered. What we found was truly a tropical paradise of trees and plants. His gardens form part of an old sugar plantation.

Established in 1680 by William Grant, his Castle Grant estate became a sizeable 272-acre sugar plantation in the

Parish of St Joseph overlooking the east coast of Barbados.

By 1913, it was owned by an Edgar Cox. During the tenure of his family a two-acre section of ground collapsed into an underground cavern forming a sizeable sink hole. This area became neglected and a dumping ground for old plantation machinery and other detritus. However, its neglect meant that many local species of fauna and flora thrived in the micro-climate of the sink hole.

In 1990 well known horticulturalist, Anthony Hunte, recognised its potential as a tropical garden that was home to the natural forest plants of Barbados. He acquired the gully and ten acres of the plantation and painstakingly set about creating a masterpiece of a tropical garden that is breath taking in its dimensions and variety of plants.

Cabbage palm trees soar over the garden and under their canopy a variety of plants thrive from anthuriums, lilies, orchids, hibiscus, euphorbia, begonias, tulip trees to well over a hundred local and international species. It's a magical place and well worth a visit.

23 May 2021

Island Life part 2

Having received our first dose of the AstraZeneca vaccine, and with 26% of the population now inoculated, we have become more adventurous in our socialising. At our golf club a Canadian couple from the UK, also here on the Welcome Stamp, have befriended us. We have formed a foursome and now play regularly together. Last week they invited us over for dinner. This is the first dinner invitation we have accepted so it was with some excitement that we smartened ourselves up and headed for Mount Standfast on the west coast where they are renting a detached house.

The area they live in is known as the platinum coast as this where the smart set and those with money live. Rihanna has a house here as does Cliff Richard and other celebrities. The area contains Sandy Lane, the premier resort on the island, which boasts three fabulous golf courses and the Royal Westmoreland resort another five-star complex with yet another beautiful golf course. Their estates are extensive and well-manicured. As we drove along, we craned our necks in all directions taking in the smart villas and lovely gardens.

Our Canadian couple have rented a large house situated on the edge of a cliff and set in two acres of gardens that also contains a cave full of bats. The trees and foliage are abundant and overlook the sea below. The house faces west and I imagine the sunsets are wonderful. They also brought their Bengal cat with them; a strikingly marked animal.

Our host, like many here, works in IT and manages largescale infrastructure projects. Dinner was a curry and we sat out on the terrace at a table by the pool taking in the expansive vista as darkness fell. It was a congenial evening but we couldn't stay late as there is still a night time curfew in place at weekends and we had a 45-minute drive home.

On our return we noticed a handful of large objects on the pathway up to our house. On closer examination these turned out to be cane toads. Massive in every respect they contain large venom sacs on their backs which can kill small mammals such as cats and dogs. Imported in the 18th century to eat sugar cane beetles and bugs, which they successfully do, they have bred in large numbers and along with monkeys and mongooses have become a pest. They invade properties looking for cat and dog food and during the day like nothing better than to dig a hole in a flower pot or flower bed to rest up causing more damage.

Apparently, there are two ways to get rid of them, spray them with a suitable insecticide or catch them, place them in containers and put them in one's fridge freezer for twenty-four hours until dead. Unless, a multitude invade us we'll leave them be and hope they move on.

Being out on the west coast we noticed a large Massy

Supermarket and decided to return and see what they had to offer. This was a new experience. Bigger than our local one at Six Roads it has an affiliation with Waitrose and the product range is much greater. Prices of many canned goods were also cheaper. We might do our main supermarket shopping there in future.

We are also moving into Hurricane season and the local media is full of precautionary steps to take when the storms arrive. So, that will be a new experience following the volcanic ash fall out.

5 June 2021

Local and Peculiar

Visitors and those interested in Barbados will know the history and interesting facts about the country; its imported wildlife, plantations, sugar, rum, the origin of its name, that George Washington stayed here and more. However, having been here five months we have noticed a few things that may not appear in the guidebooks and that are peculiar to the island so I thought I would set down some of our observations here.

A door to nowhere - there is one peculiar feature that we have noticed time and again that forms part of many properties.

That is a door set up high in an outside wall with no steps or balcony to walk out onto. We cannot see the logic and despite asking locals receive no satisfactory reply. Strange.

Patience – Bajans are a patient people and rather than cause a situation they will wait for something to happen. Here's an example. Sitting on a bus full of people, the driver decides to sit under a tree reading a paper and eating a snack. Many minutes go by and we all sit patiently waiting. It's hot and there is no AC in the bus. The bus should have left 15 minutes ago. The driver seems unconcerned. Eventually, a young woman, smartly dressed, has had enough. 'Are we going to stand for this?' she addresses the bus. 'Well, are we?' The seated throng begin to grumble a reluctant 'No!' The woman warms to her theme and when she feels she has our support she steps down from the bus and harangues the driver. He looks up startled, folds his paper, packs up his picnic and steps with alacrity into the bus and behind the wheel. Everyone is shouting now. The bus driver puts his foot down and we career down the potholed road as he tries to make up time.

The national dish – the traditional national dish is Cou Cou and Flying Fish. However, most locals will tell you it's now Chefette. Chefette is the local equivalent of McDonalds. Every outlet always has a huge queue of cars snaking down the road and its products are consumed by all sectors of the population.

The murder rate – for a small country the murder rate is on the higher side, 0.02% of the population annually compared to say the UK at 0.001%.

Historically, murders were committed mainly with knives but the American underworld has begun to realise that there is ready market here for guns ranging from handguns to AK 47s. There are over 10,000 guns on the island of which only 3,000 are registered. The issue regularly dominates the news in our local papers. Having said this, Barbados is considerably safer than many Caribbean

islands and the criminal fraternity are general the targets.

Car cemetery – I've commented on this before but the island is littered with wrecks but these wrecks are not deposited in the countryside but are kept on the yards of people's homes. Cars and spare parts for them are expensive here. Once a car has finally done enough miles, destroyed its suspension on the roads and suffered the ravages of the sun its 'retired' to the family yard and provides an ongoing source of spares from light bulbs to bits of bodywork until it has been totally cannibalised whereupon the carcass just sits to be consumed by creepers and weeds.

Mosquitoes – In the Far East and elsewhere I have been bitten numerous times by mosquitoes but in those parts of the world I have generally been aware of their presence through their size and the particular audible sound they make and they are easy to see and deal with. In Barbados we seem to have a silent assassin variety that is hard to see and makes no discernible noise. You only realise you have become a victim sometime later when the skin begins to itch. They are hard to see and swat. I did some research to see if I could track down the local strain. It appears that out of the thousands of species of mosquito in the world only three of them exist in Barbados - the Culex, the Anopheles and the Aedes Aegypti. It's the last which is our culprit and is the most common here. It's small, between 1.80mm and 3mm in size and most commonly feeds indoors at dusk and dawn. This is the species that can spread dengue fever so we have to be alert and ensure as dusk falls, we close our outer doors, ensure screens are in place and have the necessary sprays, coils, plug in deterrents and citronella candles handy.

Grape fruit - I hadn't realised that the grapefruit originated in Barbados. The pink grapefruits here are wonderful in taste but I use them in a cocktail with ice and Campari!

To finish this subject. I have also noted a couple of facts that may not be so widely known.

Barbados, before it was occupied by the British, had a population of thousands of wild pigs! How did they get here? Apparently, the Portuguese, who predated Britain's arrival in Barbados, left several pigs to breed ready for the day when they would return. The British were the lucky recipients of a ready supply of pork and bacon.

Finally, Barbados was the only holiday destination in the world to be privileged enough to receive scheduled flights from Concord. During the years Concord flew, it made more than 7,000 flights here between 1987 and 2003. The average flying time was three hours and 45 minutes compared to eight hours and 30 minutes today. Only 20 Concordes were ever manufactured. The 12th, a British Airways plane which flew here, is on display at a museum located beside the island's main international airport – Grantley Adams.

18 June 2021

Hurricane season

We are now in hurricane season and while Barbados is thankfully on the edge of the area that feels the full force of hurricanes, we still feel the effects. Two nights ago, we endured our first savage tropical storm. The winds rose to a howling intensity accompanied by driving rain, loud claps of thunder and continuous sheet lightning. According to the local weather centre we averaged 490 lightning strikes per minute with an incredible 46,290 lightning strikes over a one-hour period. It was like being at a rock concert without the music. The power went off after ten minutes but that didn't matter as it was 2.00 in the morning.

I was expecting to see some devastation in the morning but all looked calm outside. Our landlady's partner Pedro, a farmer, came by and said as much as we needed the rain the intensity wasn't good for his newly planted crops. He's proving to be a useful contact as he brings us fresh fruit, veg and meat at less than supermarket prices.

It's mango season and the trees across the island are fully laden with the fruit and the heady scent they give off. The monkeys love them. But they are not available in the supermarkets which is strange. I'm guessing they are not commercially grown here and that local roadside sellers pick them and sell them on their stalls, which they do. So, mangoes now form part of our daily diet.

In terms of daily life, apart from mask wearing, Covid seems almost a memory. There have only been 47 deaths in total and apart from a handful of positive cases, a two-week lockdown in February and a period of evening curfew things here have been normal for the last few months. We have got a little lax and have to ensure we keep hand sanitising and maintaining a distance when out shopping. We are scheduled to receive our second Covid jab this Sunday.

From an economic perspective, tourists are few and far between, and, those with second properties here who come for the winter months from the UK, Europe and Americas, have returned home so the island feels quite quiet. Lawrence Gap, Oistins and the west coast, popular visitor areas and normally buzzing with people. are quiet and we have the place almost to ourselves.

Swimming is a problem though. Vast amounts of sargassum (seaweed) have invaded the popular beaches from the Atlantic to the east and the sea is a nasty green as a result. So, we have had to drive a fair way up the west coast to find beaches where the Caribbean Sea and beaches are clear. We drove up the road leading to the Colony Club, a top hotel, the barrier was raised, some advantages to looking like a tourist, and we spent an afternoon on the beach in front of this luxurious hotel. I only counted three people within their complex on sun loungers.

It's amazing how you get used to what's on your

doorstep. In our first six weeks here, we were on the beach almost every day enjoying the sunshine, the azure sea and wonderful sunsets but then we lost the tourist mentality realising of course that this wonderful facility was available anytime.

As my consultancy work with an organisation in the UK has fallen away due to Covid, I have now written and published my fourth murder mystery 'Death at Ballard's Mill'. Set in Barbados the series tracks the experiences of a DCI Wayne Johnson as he strives to solve different murders.

Having said this, we are now trying to deliver presentations via Adobe Connect. So, I'm hoping to be able to continue my work remotely delivering presentations to employers once we have this system up and running and clients signed up.

11 July 2021

Storm Elsa strikes!

In the early hours of Friday, the 2nd of July, the tail end of tropical storm Elsa passed over Barbados developing into a Category 1 hurricane (the lowest and least severe) as it cleared the island.

We awoke to winds of around 50mph (80 kph) occasionally gusting to 75 mph (120 kph) which by mid-morning had abated. Not much more than a brisk breeze I thought to myself used to regular storms of similar intensity that pass across East Sussex in the UK where I was living before coming here. However, the impact was severe. No water for a day. No cell reception for three days and no power for a week. We were effectively cut off from the outside world for this passage of time. 4% of the population are still without power and not expecting reconnection to the electricity grid for another week.

Was it just me or was my severe irritation at this state of affairs shared by my neighbours? They felt the same way. How could a developing nation like Barbados, often dubbed the 'Singapore of the Caribbean', become effectively paralysed by the passing of a tropical storm in an area which yearly endures a hurricane season? Various government and business luminaries in the media are wittering on about crisis preparedness, the plans they have in place to deal with such eventualities and what is being done to fix the problems of lack of power, collapsed wooden houses and the homeless.

It seems to me they are all missing the point particularly when it comes to power. This is all about preventative maintenance and having an up to date and robust infrastructure in place to deal with annual storms and hurricanes. Apparently, more than 500 telegraph poles fell over and over 40 transformers destroyed. How can this be? How can this kind of damage be sustained in winds of moderate intensity? It surely comes down to management - bad management and inefficiency.

The island's power infrastructure is carried on wooden telegraph poles, many of which look past their sell-by date and carrying a bewildering array of cables. The average life of a wooden pole is between 25 to 50 years depending on the harshness of the climate and terrain. I wonder how old most of the existing stock of poles on the island is? Someone in government needs to be taking the power company to task and be asking searching questions about their maintenance programme otherwise this kind of occurrence is going to become common.

Many of us are here on the Welcome Stamp, a 12-month visa programme, enticing us to come and work remotely in paradise utilising a modern IT and communications infrastructure. Not being able to communicate with employers and clients for a week or more is not exactly what we signed up for particularly when we paid a not insubstantial sum to take advantage of the programme plus moving costs. I hope the CEO of the Tourist Board will be asking the same questions. Otherwise, God help us if a severe hurricane strikes the island.

11 July 2021

Summer Holiday

Not the 1963 Cliff Richards film but a holiday for Antonina's daughters who have arrived for a three-week holiday with us. They had to quarantine for six days.

But the inefficiency of Barbados reared its head again. They had no wifi. I was told by the hotel that the cell network (Digicel) in the area was down. Funny, I thought, as the wifi in the café attached to the hotel was working perfectly. I checked in the hotel across the road and theirs was working too – both on the Digicel network. I confronted the hotel manager who gave me the same blarney. I mentioned this and started discussing a 50% refund as how could two young women, one a student, be cooped up for six days unable to communicate with the outside world? One had studying to do. This had a magical effect. Within two hours a wifi extender was supplied to their room and they could communicate!

Once out of the hotel, the girls, not surprisingly, wanted to hit the beach.

Unfortunately, our favoured locations are blighted with sargassum. This forced us to find a new beach and we discovered Brownes beach; the best beach on the island they say.

The sea was clear and the seabed a gently shelving base of white sand. We took to the water. I was a little way out when two guys on the shore began to wave frantically at me pointing to the sea behind. A large dark object was moving menacingly towards me. I needed no second warning. It's been a long time since I swam freestyle competitively, I swam for Surrey in my youth and was a champion swimmer, and I covered the fifty yards back to the beach in record time. It was a sting ray; some five feet across. It came to within a couple of feet of the shore and swam lazily along the edge. They are not normally dangerous to humans but they carry a long wicked looking poisonous tail and I remembered it was just such a creature that killed the botanist and adventurer Steve Irwin.

After that excitement we settled down on our loungers when a local approached us asking if we would like to swim with the turtles, look at a coral reef and the multitude of coloured fish that inhabited it; a one-hour boat trip. 'How much?' I asked. USD 40 each came the reply. I declined. A family from Boston just along from us took up his offer and we watched with interest where the speed boat took them. Just four hundred yards offshore. In the afternoon, we donned goggles and swam out to where the boat had been and saw turtles, small sting rays and lots of fish; keeping a weather eye out for the big sting ray!

We took the girls on a half day tour of the eastern side of

the island and saw St John's cathedral, a pretty 1837 church; it's earlier 1645 incarnation having been destroyed in a hurricane.

The graveyard contained some interesting people.

We visited an old sugar cane plantation high up in the hills where the 18th century owner was expecting his first child. The child was born and turned out to be black! Unable to live with this he rode his horse off the edge of a cliff; poor horse and poor family.

We saw the only working windmill on the island but it was closed.

We ventured onto a cliffs edge on the east coast and down some steps cut of the coral.

I spied a large rusting iron bollard on a large platform of flat rock. Apparently, after the slave trade was made illegal by Britain, illicit slave ships used to dock here for supplies en route to the Americas. The then plantation owner, whose land encompassed this landing point, was happy to provide victuals and fresh water in return for suitable recompense. The spot is situated in a desolate part of the coast, well away from the prying eyes of the local British authorities of the time.

We finished the day with a swam on a more turbulent east coast beach.

We also revisited the lovely west coast beach by the Colony Club hotel. The sea was clear and calm and we rediscovered our joy of spending time on a beach and in the sea promising ourselves we must do this at least once a week once the girls have returned home.

19 July 2021

Birthday at Sandy Lane GC

Yesterday was Antonina's birthday and she chose to spend it at Sandy Lane golf club with a round of golf on their Country Club course followed by lunch on the clubhouse terrace overlooking the course and the sea.

What a place and what an estate. Everything is well-manicured and the service is friendly and excellent. This is golfing at the premier level from a concierge service the moment you arrive to modern golf carts equipped with GPS so you know all the yardages you need to know, ice box with ice and cold bottles of water, a folder containing branded tees, ball marker and divot repair tool and hot and cold running towels!

The assistant in the pro's shop suggested we might like to try the Green Monkey course. This is an exclusive course

normally reserved for hotel guests only. But, with the economic downturn visitors have the opportunity to play it. There was a catch. A round would cost USD 4,000 each! After choking back what might have been a rude exclamation and recovering my poise, I said we'd stick to the Country Club course.

The course is in excellent condition with fairways as good as most greens. A caddy comes with the round and he pointed out the best lines to take and cleaned clubs between shots as well as repairing divot marks. On several holes the views out over the Caribbean Sea were breath taking. It was hard to concentrate on the golf.

All too soon we were back in the clubhouse and taking our ease on the terrace having a drink before we ordered lunch. The lunch was excellent and the staff produced a cake with a candle and sang happy birthday.

We could get used to this kind of life.

The Sandy Lane hotel estate came into being in 1961 after a British politician Ronald Tree was inspired to create a luxury hotel with a golf course on the island using land that was originally the old Sandy Lane sugar plantation. It quickly became known as the only truly elegant, sophisticated and chic hotel in Barbados and the Caribbean.

Sold to the Trust house group in the late sixties its future was in doubt when new owners Granada in the nineties felt the hotel didn't fit its profile. A group of Irish businessmen stepped in and acquired the property with the aim of creating the most distinguished address in the Caribbean and elevating hotel luxury to a whole new level. The hotel closed in 1998 for refurbishment.

An underground engineering plant was installed to accommodate all back of house services including a desalination plant. A new Spa and pool were put in and 45 holes of world championship golf, with two courses designed by Tom Fazio, were constructed. The hotel re-opened in 2001.

It is, indeed, a hotel worthy of its five stars and I love their current branding with pink the dominant colour.

August 2021

An English Summer

After seven months in Barbados, I have had to return to the UK for a family matter. I was looking forward to seeing how things had changed. On arrival, many things seem familiar. The weather is grim, 15 C and raining in Eastbourne, our test cricket team are failing with the bat, the royalty continues to be rocked by allegations of impropriety from Prince Andrew and fuel prices continue to increase.

On a brighter note, I have never seen the countryside look more verdant, due to a combination of periodic hot sunshine and lots of rain, life seems normal as most Covid restrictions have been lifted and it's good to be able to visit a country pub and drink a pint of Old Bodgers.

But I'm getting ahead of myself. First, I had to negotiate the return trip. I booked a VIP testing package from the

Crane Hotel in Barbados to take my outbound PCR test. The Crane is reputedly one of the top hotels in Barbados. The marketing blurb states 'set on Barbados' beautiful South East coast, the oldest operating hotel (since 1887) in the Caribbean has effortlessly married the old-world charm of its past, to all the 21st-century amenities and services expected by today's most discerning travellers. The Crane Resort overlooks the pink sands and turquoise waters of Crane Beach - one of the top 10 beaches in the world.'

Hmm, I thought, as I had a coffee overlooking the beach while I awaited my test results. The pink sands are covered in a thick, broad layer of sargassum (seaweed) which was rotting nicely on the beach under a hot sun. The smell was indescribable. If I was a paying guest, I wouldn't be a happy bunny.

But the Covid service was efficient and I had avoided the queues at the public facility in Bridgetown.

The second thing I had to do was to book my day two test in the UK after arrival. Barbados, thankfully, is on the Green List so this meant no quarantine. The company I picked would post this to me and I would self-administer the test and return it in a pre-paid envelope.

I flew British Airways and the flight was painless and uneventful. I had heard horror stories of the queues at Heathrow but these appeared unfounded. The only glitch was that the biometric passport booths were only recognising about 5% of travellers' passports. No matter, I was soon out and, in a taxi, heading to Eastbourne.

That first night I had my first pint of real ale in seven months and complemented it with an Indian takeaway. Heaven!

The next thing I did was to venture out onto an English golf course. I have never seen golf courses here in such good shape. The fairways are green and firm and the greens are in excellent condition. I'll pack as much golf as I can into the trip.

Mask wearing is no longer obligatory though all shops and stores advise you to wear a mask on entry. Having got used to mandatory mask-wearing in Barbados I found it no hardship but about fifty percent of customers are not wearing masks. With the Delta variant running riot here I found this surprising.

After seven months of sunshine and warmth, I found the British climate hard to adjust too so much so that on the first two days I had to put on the central heating. Mid-summer in the UK this is not.

I travelled up to the Midlands to stay with a friend who lives in a medieval abbey and to visit my brother and sister.

On the return trip I encountered the usual August traffic madness on the MI; two separate multi-car pile-ups on both carriageways on either side of Leicester Forest East service station. I spent an hour sitting on the Central reservation chatting to a sales rep for a health and wellbeing company. A couple of cockney likely lads in a panel van on the opposite carriageway shouted across 'You'll need sleeping bags mate. Horrendous accident in front of you. Could be hours clearing it away.' My heart sank. Fortunately, we were on the move within ten minutes. Bloody cockney jokers, I thought to myself smiling.

But overall, it's good to be back. However, I am looking forward to returning to the blue skies and sunshine of the Caribbean.

30 August 2021

Return to Barbados

All too soon, it was time to pack up and return to Barbados. I had enjoyed my three weeks in England catching up with family and friends plus playing some golf. The temperature rarely rose about 18 degrees though I did enjoy some sunny days and managed to lower the hood on my convertible sports BMW and enjoy the feel of English countryside air.

Amid the gloom, there was another ray of sunshine. The English test cricket team had finally managed to get their act together and with a superb display of bowling and batting had routed the Indians at Headingly levelling the series at 1 all.

Negotiating the return covid protocols and online

booking system for BA presented some challenges. I was tested at a facility in Brighton two days before I flew but the result was still not back on the evening before my flight. I phoned and luckily got through to a human who assured me I would receive the certificate within five minutes by email. An hour and a half later I was still waiting. Was I negative or positive? If positive I would have to rearrange my flight at the eleventh hour. I was somewhat stressed. I made another phone call and waited while the guy at the other end emailed me my result. I was negative and could now fill out the necessary online Barbados covid form plus their customs and immigration forms. I then completed the online check-in with BA and fell into bed relieved.

Unlike our trip out in January and my return trip three weeks earlier, Heathrow was buzzing.

Pent-up demand for a holiday in the sunshine had, evidently, been released. My flight was full of Brits seeking the blue skies and beaches of Barbados. Barbados airport was a zoo as our flight coincided with two others from the UK and the US. Fortunately, my concierge VIP testing package from the Crane came into its own. I was met on the tarmac by a smartly dressed young man with a placard bearing my name and he whisked me through the fast-track channel for covid checking and customs and immigration.

Within forty-five minutes I was in the testing facility at the Crane Hotel being swabbed for my PCR test. I had read that the result would be delivered within the hour but was told it could take until midnight! What was I supposed to do until then? Enjoy the hotel's facilities came the reply which I found a bit bizarre, having free rein to roam the premises possibly infecting other guests.

I rang Antonina and asked her to join me for dinner which she did. I was then reminded by her that the overnight curfew was still in place and she had to be back home before 11 pm. At 10 pm with no result in sight, I decided to leave the hotel and together we travelled home. No problem leaving the precincts of the hotel and I collapsed into bed exhausted.

The result finally came at 9 am the following morning. If I had followed the guidelines, I guess I would have had to sleep on a pool lounger or take a room, which wasn't the idea behind the Jetsetter VIP package I had booked. No matter, I was negative and can now readjust to life back here.

It is good to be back in the sunshine and warmth and wake up to blue skies!

14 September 2021

Hot, Hot, Hot!

The locals tell us September is the hottest month. They are not wrong. The mercury hovers around 32 degrees C and it can be hotter inside where rooms face the sun. Coincidentally, the fresh breeze, a constant the rest of the year, has died away which intensifies the heat.

Like the locals, we are adapting to getting up early and going for walks or playing golf in the hours between 6.30 am and 9.30 am before the heat from the sun begins to take effect. We do the same early evening.

We tend to siesta in the afternoons, something as a family we used to do in India.

The problems with incoming sargassum or seaweed have abated and we can visit our favourite local beaches without having to tread through the stuff, smell it or swim in it. The sea is back to its clear, azure blue best.

There are more tourists but they couldn't have picked a hotter month to visit. They are easily identifiable on the beaches by the deep pink of their bodies where not enough factor 50 has been applied.

We are being bitten more too, at dusk and dawn, as small sandflies add their predatory peregrinations to those of the local mosquitoes. We spray our legs and arms liberally with repellents that bear apposite names like 'Off' and 'Go'.

Like the UK, Barbados has also enjoyed a lot of rain in recent weeks and it has transformed the island into patchworks of verdant green making parts of it resemble the countryside one can find in France and England.

As a result, our efforts at gardening are bearing fruit and all the cuttings 'acquired' from the golf clubs, roadsides and abandoned lots are turning into small shrubs and flowers. It turns out that Antonina, who has never gardened before, has green fingers and reads voraciously online about the plants involved, what to do, where they should be sited and so on. She's a natural gardener and plantsman. Cacti and succulents which grow well here have become an area of expertise.

As for me, I am virtually a full-time writer as consultancy

work with my client organisation in the UK has fallen away.

Even though I think my knowledge of the English language is good and that I write coherently I have started to use a writing editor called Grammarly, a cross-platform cloud-based writing assistant that reviews spelling, grammar, punctuation, clarity, engagement, and delivery mistakes. I always knew Ukraine was another Silicon Valley in terms of its IT expertise and it came as no surprise to find that the platform was launched in 2009 by three Ukrainians with their head office now in San Francisco.

It also provides feedback and their latest email tells me I am more productive and have a greater mastery of English and use of vocabulary than 99% of users. Some comfort, but then maybe for those who tend to use it English is not their first language. Still, if you are a budding writer, I would recommend it.

I am now deep in a Victorian love story set in the Empire around 1897 and 1898. The heroine is an English girl who falls in love with a maverick Hussar officer who sees action in Afghanistan and Uganda.

I am enjoying doing the background research and discovering that British survey teams were uncovering tracts of land and tribes in East Africa that despite the long presence of German, French and British traders, missionaries and colonial administrators had never seen a white man before. But two local rulers unite to rid themselves of the British, and Uganda in 1897 was at boiling point as we struggled to hang onto the fledgling East African Protectorate.

Troops from India were drafted in to resolve the situation so along with the Zulu and Boer wars plenty was happening in the late nineteenth century on the dark continent, a term coined by the Victorian explorer Henry Stanley because it was unexplored by Europeans and for the savagery they expected to find there. Whether we should have been there in the first place is something for the revisionists to discuss but history is history.

7 October 2021

October and all change

We have completed nine months here and the weather has changed. September was a hot month with no breeze and then October arrived. As if switching on a light, the winds returned, the rain came and it's a couple of degrees cooler. For which we are very thankful.

The monkeys have returned and made themselves at home on the balcony of the vacant house opposite gaining entry through a tear in the plastic mesh screening. The bonnet of our car acts as a natural platform for the youngsters who view the windscreen wipers with curiosity and objects to be pulled and snapped back!

Our plants and flowers have also benefited from the rain.

September was also a record month in terms of Covid. A 50% increase in total deaths was recorded for September and we are now running at 200 positive cases a day. There is no explanation in the media as to why this should be. More tourists are visiting the island and we know of one person who boarded the plane here from the UK with a negative PCR test only to fall ill on arrival and be tested positive. No doubt her family, who were travelling with her, will also be affected.

The situation is not helped by the unvaccinated here avoiding inoculation. 38% of the total population is now vaccinated but there seems to be a reluctance among the rest largely because of fear of possible side effects. The PM has insisted her government will not issue a formal decree compelling people to be vaccinated as it goes against the spirit of current legislation and human rights. Business leaders are now taking things into their own hands. Digicel, the largest mobile phone service provider, has insisted all employees must show evidence of vaccination. This has caused some debate in the media.

The hospitality trade is adopting a similar stance. Given we are a tourist-based economy something has to be done. As a result of all this, we are back to being super cautious in our mixing with people and avoid large gatherings.

The snowbirds are also beginning to return to their winter homes here as the weather becomes colder in Canada. This will help the local economy though our ease in obtaining tee times at the golf club will be impacted!

We have also come across a fruit new to us – the Ackee (*Blighia sapida*). The fruit is a mixed blessing. Though originally native to West Africa, it migrated to Jamaica in 1778 and subsequently other Caribbean islands. The scientific name honours Captain William Bligh who took the fruit from Jamaica to the Royal Botanic Gardens in Kew, England, in 1793. It is considered Jamaica's national fruit. If improperly eaten, though, ackee can cause a vomiting sickness, which can lead to coma or death. Unripe ackee fruit contains a poison called hypoglycin, so one needs to wait until the fruit's protective pods turn red and open naturally. Once open, the only edible portion is the yellow arilli, which surround the toxic black seeds.

It's an interesting looking fruit but I think I'll give it a miss!

16 November 2021

It's all monkey business

Both literally and figuratively.

By literally, I mean monkeys are becoming an increasing menace to farmers and householders. I was sitting at my desk when I heard a chattering outside. I looked up and saw a monkey hop onto our verandah balustrade, look at me, then pluck two rosebuds off a rose in a pot and pop them in his mouth. They must be tasty. He then leapt back into a tree as I came outside to remonstrate. Ten minutes later five of them invaded the verandah and I couldn't understand why the attention until I realised, I had a fruit bowl on the coffee table that contain oranges and bananas. They must be scenting the bananas. I immediately removed them and put them in a cupboard.

Next door neighbour's dog, who spends all day with us, just slept through the whole affair. I gave her a nudge and she leapt into action barking and chasing them off into the road.

As for the farmers, monkeys are a real pest. I spoke with Pedro, who is my landlady's partner and a farmer, and he says they are a real menace. His solution is to weave newspaper among his crops which rustle in the wind. The monkeys don't appear to like this.

I might do the same but think I will invest in a high-power water pistol which worked well against wild dogs in the Algarve when I had a house there.

As for figuratively, on 30 November 1966, Barbados became an independent state and Commonwealth realm with Elizabeth II as its Head of State. On the 30th of November this year we become a Republic. Sandra Mason, the current British appointed Governor General, has been appointed to become the first president of Barbados. On 30 November 2021, she will replace Queen Elizabeth as Head of State. So, a major change.

The population is largely apathetic about this transition but those who have position and influence are worried that the prime minister, Mia Mottley, is making a grab for longer lasting power. And they question whether this move is in the interests of Barbados and feel its suits the interests of Mia Mottley. She is a powerful personality and leader who is moving onto the world stage, latterly at the climate change conference. It's a load of monkey business they reckon.

As for those of us here on the Welcome Stamp, I guess we will just keep on doing what we are doing, enjoy the sunshine, the beaches and the laid-back lifestyle.

We are now moving into high season and the tourists are returning in droves which is good for local businesses. In tandem with this the government has relaxed the curfew hours and instead of 9 pm we can now party until midnight! Tourists, locals and businesses are liking this. Another plus for Mottley. She has the populist touch even if the number of covid cases and deaths are rising.

The heat of September has passed and the winter trade winds have returned so things are a cooler, though that's relative as the mercury hovers at 28/29 C during the day, though this is better than 34 C! No need for AC or fans which is also good news. I still exist in just a pair of shorts around the house which is good news as far as I am concerned.

I have found a pretty place to breakfast in with its own private beach and after a round of golf at 6.30 in the morning, breakfast there, before a swim, home and a siesta. I do this three times a week. What's not to like? I've fully embraced this lifestyle and won't miss the British winter!

25 December 2021

Christmas Bajan style

Barbados is closed for three days as the Bajans celebrate Christmas; that is apart from the tourist hotels and outlets which serve them as they are a 24/7 operation. Even the ice cream vans with their annoying jingle which never seems to change have ceased to ply their daily trade thank goodness. Barbados is a nation of churchgoers but we decided not to attend midnight mass on Christmas Eve or the morning Christmas service today. Covid is readily transmissible in the churches here as congregations enjoy lustily singing their hymns and gospels.

Pockets of the island are ablaze with Christmas decorations and lights including some of the churches. Many homes have external Christmas decorations with cacti substituted for fir trees.

We decided to begin our Christmas Day with a visit to the Colony Club beach on the west coast, our favourite, have a coffee in the five-star Coral Reef hotel followed by a swim in the sea and a lie back under some palm trees.

Unlike previous visits when the beach and the hotels were empty, they were full of tourists sunning themselves, swimming, sailing Hobie cats and water skiing. The hotels must be delighted with the uptake in tourist traffic and associated income. Luckily there is enough space to be able to find a quiet piece of sand and sea.

The water was calm, clear and around 26 degrees; perfect. Much like natural baths found in spa resorts many locals believe the Caribbean Sea has healing properties. Perhaps it's all in the mind but I am ready to take that on board as I always feel better after an extended dip.

Curfew was suspended on Christmas Eve which allowed Bajans to visit restaurants, bars, their friends and party all night which may partly explain why the island appeared empty as we drove across it today. Few cars on the road and no one in sight. Maybe they were nursing hangovers or were all inside getting ready to tuck into roast turkey, ham and all the trimmings.

I am fully expecting a surge in Covid cases in one to two weeks' time as families and friends have been congregating but the government is being realistic and will cope with whatever arises. Unlike many countries, we are fortunate that life continues pretty much as normal here apart from mask-wearing and the nightly curfew between midnight and 5.00 am.

Being a small island on the Eastern edge of the Caribbean has its advantages as one can only get here by air and those who embark on a flight here have to have a negative PCR test. As a result, Omicron has yet to reach our shores. Though no doubt it will arrive at some point.

It's the best time of year weatherwise too. The sun shines but daytime temperatures are around 27 degrees falling to 22/23 at night. And it's not so humid; a marked contrast to the hot summer months. This slight shift in climate is also noticeable in the fauna and flora as deciduous trees have shed leaves and evergreens look a lot less luxuriant. Even the monkeys have disappeared perhaps holed up in their jungle domains enjoying a Christmas diet of bananas that grow plentifully here in the wild.

Well, it's cocktail hour so time to open some bubbly and finish preparing the Christmas roast for this evening's Christmas dinner; lamb for a change.

3 January 2022

And so, we enter a new year

We have been here almost exactly a year. We left with covid raging across the UK and finish the year with the arrival of the Omicron variant in Barbados.

The country's CMO has confirmed one case. Like elsewhere, we are being advised to get our booster vaccinations and for those not vaccinated to step forward. He went on to add 'Covid-19 will be with us for the long-term. We want to make it more like dealing with the flu. We have to live with the hand we have been dealt.' All sensible stuff.

Meanwhile, the PM sprang a surprise on Boxing Day

announcing a snap General Election on January the 19th. This caught opposition parties on the hop with the announcement coming amid the holiday season. One editorial likened it to receiving a Curtley Ambrose yorker!

Inevitably cries of unfairness at the lack of time to prepare rang out but as another commentator put it 'I don't know which world them living in, but part of the strategy of calling a snap election is to catch opposing parties unaware. Isn't it in the bible that the Lord says 'Behold, I come as a thief in the night. Blessed is he that watcheth and keepeth his garments on''? Quite so.

Yet more commentators think this is all part of some grand plan hatched by the PM that began with us becoming a Republic, which in their opinion was sold to the populace as a simple 'cosmetic change.' A referendum should have been called though the constitution doesn't demand it. According to a poll, Bajans haven't taken kindly to not being consulted. They fear we are now on the road to a dictatorship. I guess only time will tell.

So, 2022 has got off to an interesting start.

Exactly a year ago yesterday we arrived in Barbados; where that time has gone, I don't know. We are set for another twelve months having taken up the government's invitation to extend our Welcome Stamp for a second year.

I can't see a reason to return to a wet UK winter, covid restrictions and Boris' fractured politics. We'll just chill in the sunshine, wear our masks when out and about, observe the social distance and carry on as normal.

17 February 2022

Molasses, money and murder

We are supposedly in the dry season but as I write the rain is hammering down again; a true tropical downpour. These downpours don't last for long but they are regular and help keep the island looking green and fertile.

The tourist trade I'm told, by those who ply their trade in this sector, is up by 50% and increasing, of its normal capacity which is encouraging. There are many more planes flying in and many more tourists on the beaches.

With this increase in tourists came two separate sets of friends from the UK who stayed in local hotels. We enjoyed showing them what we know of the island.

One attraction which we had not visited before was St Nicholas Abbey. Not an abbey at all but a sugar plantation dating back to the 1650s. It's a rarity in that it has maintained its exact boundaries since that time; surrounding some four hundred acres.

The estate has a vivid history worthy of a murder mystery. The original owners, two British partners, Colonel Benjamin Berringer and John Yeamans, competed for the affections of one Margaret, the beguiling daughter of a local reverend. Colonel Benjamin Berringer prevailed and they married and had three children.

Some years later, in May of 1661, the good colonel set off from the plantation to dine with an old friend in in Speightstown, a busy seaport on the west coast, leaving Margaret with the three children at home.

During the meal he clasped his throat, cried out, vomited on the floor and died. Poisoning was the verdict. John Yeamans was the main suspect but the case against him remained unproven. No local Hercule Poirot in those days!

Yeamans and Margaret were married within ten weeks of her husband's death. He was never brought to justice and continued to lead a colourful life being knighted by Charles II for his loyalty and offered the appointment as Governor General of Carolina which was a single colony at the time.

This appointment came with 48,000 acres of land so Yeamans and Margaret uprooted and with a coffle of slaves set off for Carolina to start up a plantation. These slaves were the first to be introduced into that colony.

Upon the death of Yeamans and Margaret the estate passed to her children. The subsequent history of the estate is just as fascinating.

Moving to the present, apart from a short interlude after 1947, St Nicholas Abbey has grown sugar cane to this day. Now, it's a working plantation that's become a micro-brewery making its own rum which they bottle and knockout in an airy room behind the house. They make their own labels, stoppers out of solid mahogany and leather plugged into beautiful bottles.

Pure single estate rum tastes similar to a cognac or whiskey; totally different to the cheap blended stuff. And the difference in taste between a 5 and an 8-year-old rum was noticeable; 8 years being very smooth on the palate. I can't imagine what the 25-year-old rum tastes like! Amazing I should think. But at USD700 a bottle I'm not likely to find out. It smelt fantastic though. Both the owner's wife and son gave us the insights; fascinating.

We looked round the house which is only one of three original Jacobean houses still standing in the Western

Hemisphere, typically period British architecture and furniture.

The owner must also be a train enthusiast as he has installed on the 400-acre estate a narrow-gauge railway with steam locomotive and carriages to evoke the days when Barbados had a train system which shifted cane and rum to the port and locals to the east coast for trade or leisure. We took the trip of around 18 minutes to a nearby lookout spot from where you could Ragged Point lighthouse close to where we reside - a clear view of 18 miles.

This day trip reminded me how much of Barbados's colourful past we have still to explore. We have all too easily slipped into a local's way of life. No doubt the visit of more friends and family from the UK will help us redress this.

27 February 2022

Russia, ruination and resistance

Sitting here in Barbados it's hard to believe that a major war is being fought once again in Europe and that a modern western nation faces ruination, as Russia invaded Ukraine on 24 February.

My partner, Antonina, is Ukrainian and like many Ukrainians overseas she's upset and feels guilty at not being able to be there to support other civilians, the military and police. In WhatsApp video chats with her family and friends we can see and hear bombs and missiles striking buildings and installations not far away from their homes in Kyiv.

Many have organised themselves into local neighbourhood watch groups in contact with army and police. Apart from watching and reporting on Russian movements the women are busy making Molotov cocktails while the men are familiarising themselves with an assortment of guns supplied by the army - surreal. Those who cannot leave and who've chosen to resist are determined to account for at least one Russian soldier each. Tragic.

Putin is reaping a legacy left behind by the Soviet Union when all children and teenagers had to join local Pioneer groups, think a combination of Girl Guides, Cubs, Scouts and Hitler Youth. That applies to all those now 45 and over. Antonina was taught how to strip, clean and reassemble an AK 47. She could do it in under one minute and hasn't forgotten how. She was also trained to shoot it. Many of her generation will have had the same experience.

The Russian military are encountering unexpectedly stiff resistance as those with this experience support their armed forces.

Ukrainians can be a divisive crowd but when faced with a common enemy they put their differences aside and are working together to attempt to repel the invader. They also share a similar sense of sardonic humour with the British when faced with adversity as many online posts show.

I'm not about to get into the reasons behind Putin's decision to invade but I thought a Japanese professor of strategic studies had it about right when he said while the

West didn't appear to see Russia's security concerns as legitimate, NATO being a defensive alliance, whether we like it or not Russia has been obsessed with such security concerns for decades. It is a matter of principle for the West not to deny the right of a sovereign state to choose to join NATO but the reality, now proven, is that by ignoring this we have Russia invading Ukraine.

I don't know how it will end but as the body bags increase back home Russian mothers will surely ask why their country is invading a neighbour that shares a similar heritage and many Russian soldiers will ask themselves what they are doing in a hell not of their making.

Let's hope some sort of peaceful settlement is arrived at before the country is obliterated which is something, I believe, Putin doesn't want or envisaged.

29 February to 28 September 2022

2022 and all that

Antonina, worried about her daughters, who are in Ukraine, has flown to Europe to meet them in Poland as they left the country just after the war began. The eldest daughter has a partner who runs an IT business with offices in Barcelona. She has decamped there. The younger daughter is now with Antonina and France has taken her in as a refugee.

The French have been very welcoming and they have settled in a village near Perpignan.

I have remained in Barbados until the situation becomes clearer and I am now helping my landlady run her car rental business.

She has decided to return to the UK for the summer and has left me in charge of the operations and logistics of running the business. This means delivering and picking up cars from visiting clients, mainly at the airport, cleaning them and ensuring they are regularly serviced and attended to. It means that I have had to curtail my golf and writing but its interesting being back at work, so to speak.

It's been an enjoyable couple of months but in May, Antonina asked whether I would join them in France. I flew out on 19 May intending to back a month later. My landlady was cool with this as most of her cars were now on long term rentals and I could pick up the business on my return.

However, once I arrived in France, it became clear to me that it was untenable for Liza, Antonina's younger daughter, to remain in France. She doesn't speak French and leaving her alone in France is not an option.

They are staying in a friend's apartment in Villeneuve-de-la-Raho, a not unattractive village just south of Perpignan. It enjoys stunning views of the Pyrenees out of one window and the Mediterranean Sea could be seen out of another.

The weather was clear, sunny and warm and I began to relax in a part of France that was unfamiliar to me. We explored the locale enjoying Collioure, a pretty seaside town, Saint-Cyprien and many other places including a couple of castle towns perched in the foothills of the Pyrenees. I truly felt I was on holiday and began to think I could live in this part of France which has still to be fully discovered by European tourists and which is much cheaper to live in than both Barbados and the UK. However, this was not practical given Brexit and the fact that none of us speak French; my school boy French not really being up to intense daily use. Besides it was Liza's future we were concerned about.

I made the decision we should seek to move Liza to the

UK under the Homes for Ukraine Scheme. She is fluent in English both spoken and written. To cut a long story short we managed to complete the necessary documentation online and we left for the UK on 13 July.

I had put back my flight to Barbados until the autumn and explained the situation to our Bajan landlady who was understanding.

A friend had driven Antonina's car out of Kyiv and into Europe so we decided to use the vehicle to enter the UK rather than fly.

It took us a day to drive up to near Calais where we would board Le Shuttle. We stayed overnight in a hotel in the seaside town of Berck-sur-Mer; a strange place that resembled a large Butlins style resort for French tourists.

The following day we boarded Le Shuttle and entered the UK without difficulty. We drove to Eastbourne to an apartment I had rented. And so, we settled into life in the UK; not something I had envisaged we would be doing a couple of months before when I was slaving away in Barbados.

Fortunately, the summer has been wonderful and the heat not dissimilar to Barbados.

Liza has settled in well and found gainful employment at an MOD facility along the coast.

It is now September and it's becoming appreciable cooler. I am already thinking of a return to Barbados but tragedy has struck as Antonina's mother has succumbed to cancer and only has a short while to live. Antonina has returned to Kyiv to be with her.

I have put off my return to Barbados and once Antonina has returned, we will discuss next steps but it looks very much like our sojourn in Barbados has come to an end.

About The Author

Simon de Wulf Simon de Wulf was born and brought up in Assam, India. His mother was a natural story teller and he was fascinated by her tales of life in India and the way she told a story. After university Simon entered the world of business and worked for one of the world's largest banks based in Hong Kong and travelled their network of branches and countries giving marketing and sales presentations. Whatever the subject he always found telling a story was the essence of a good presentation.

Simon has now turned his attention to writing fiction. His first book, 'Siegfried & the Vikings' was published in 2020. His next five books, a series of murder mysteries, 'Death at Ragged Point', 'Death at Drax Hall', 'Death at Peak Bay', Death at Ballard's Mill' and 'Death on the Coast' were published in 2021. This book is the sixth in that series. He has also published a historical fiction novel, a Victorian romance, 'the Lady and the Maverick'.

Simondewulf.com

Praise For Author

Death at Ragged Point - This book was a very enjoyable read, with plot twists right until the end. Can't wait to read the next one!

Thoroughly enjoyable. A well thought out murder mystery. Would recommend it.

Siegfried & the Vikings - I enjoyed reading the book as an adult so I imagine for a child it would be just as exciting and compelling. The story was easy to follow and was well written and I can quite easily see many adventures ahead

Source: Amazon reviews

Books By This Author

Siegfried & the Vikings

One day young Siegfried is fetching water from the river when he receives the fright of his life! A fierce dragon's head looms through the mist in front of him. The mist clears revealing a longship containing more than forty grim-looking men, covered in chain mail, hefting swords and battleaxes. Who are these men? Why are they here? Siegfried discovers that they are Vikings from Norway and is so fascinated by these warriors and their leader, Odo the Dragon Slayer, that he stows away with them on their departure. Little did Siegfried know that his life was about to change forever! This is a story of how one young boy, with natural abilities and a nose for treachery, saves the Vikings and finds favour and acceptance with Odo the Dragon Slayer and his mighty warriors.

Death at Ragged Point

Sir Peter Carter, a British billionaire businessman, is found dead at his Barbados residence. Dying of cancer was not unexpected. Given his prominence, the Commissioner of Police wants to be sure he died of natural causes. DCI Wayne Johnson is tasked to investigate. He discovers that Sir Peter was murdered but uncovering the motive and proving who killed him taxes all his skills. His investigation leads him into the Colombian drug world, international money laundering and family conflicts.

Death at Drax Hall

Immi Drax, legendary reggae, rap and hip-hop star dies of Covid complications. The autopsy suggests otherwise and the investigation into his death lands on the desk of DCI Wayne Johnson.

A musical genius and philanthropist the public face of Immi Drax belies the physically aggressive and violent man he was with a history of abuse and drug use.

DCI Wayne Johnson patiently tries to uncover the truth as he and his team are drawn into the murky world of the music business, deviant behaviour and internecine family relationships.

Death at Peak Bay

A man is found shot on Peak Bay beach. With forty-plus murders a year in Barbados this is not unusual. But his shooting has all the hallmarks of a professional hit. DCI Wayne Johnson begins to investigate. He discovers that there are at least two suspects with a motive for revenge, but proof is elusive. The case is complicated with the involvement of a turf war between rival drug gangs and the appearance of a body that is linked to one of London's main crime syndicates. It takes some ingenuity on the part of DCI Wayne Johnson to uncover the real killer.

Death at Ballard's Mill

A female tourist is found dead in the pool of a picturesque boutique hotel one early morning. She appears to have drowned but the post mortem says otherwise. All indications are she was murdered. She is one of a party of six on a reunion holiday. All six had worked together for many years in their twenties and early thirties, formed binding friendships and kept in touch. The cause of death remains a mystery and DCI Wayne Johnson is drawn into a world of conflicting collegial relationships made over thirty years before. Unravelling the mystery behind her death and identifying the killer is no easy task as the clues lie deep in the past.

Death on the Coast

Three women are killed in a matter of days in a similar manner. It appears the Barbados police have a serial killer on their hands. With no clues and no leads to follow DCI Wayne Johnson and DS Danika Bayne have to draw on all their experience to identify the killer. Their analysis draws them into the world of surfing; Barbados is host to a challenger tournament, part of the world series. Could the killer be a professional surfer? DS Danika Bayne takes the lead on their enquiries and puts herself in danger before the killer is finally unmasked.

The Lady and the Maverick

It's 1897 and the lady Hermione Deloitte of Wychfield in Sussex falls in love with a young Hussar officer, Captain Charles Black. Her guardians, her aunt and uncle, do not approve of the match. Charles is posted to Afghanistan and is listed as missing in action, presumed dead. Hermione grieves and falls into despair. She meets Thomas Trollope, a young barrister, who falls in love with and woos her. Hermione eventually accepts his proposal of marriage. Charles, alive, returns to England after many adventures where he discovers Hermione is to be married. Is he too late to prevent the wedding and reclaim his lost love?

+44 2082394010.
under £500 keep receipts

Printed in Great Britain
by Amazon